Wild
TEXAS

A Celebration of Our State's Natural Beauty

Text and Photography by Richard Reynolds
Foreword by Victor Emanuel

Voyageur Press

Edited by Kari Cornell and Jeni Henrickson
Designed by Andrea Rud
Printed in China

05   06   07   08   09   5   4   3   2   1

Library of Congress Cataloging-in-Publication Data
Reynolds, Richard, 1950–
    Wild Texas : a celebration of our state's natural beauty / text and photography by Richard Reynolds ; foreword by Victor Emanuel.
        p. cm.
    Includes bibliographical references (p. 156) and index.
    ISBN 0-89658-682-0 (hardback)
    1. Natural history—Texas. I. Title.
    QH105.T4R49 2005
    508.764'022'2—dc22
                                    2005003968

Distributed in Canada by Raincoast Books
9050 Shaughnessy Street, Vancouver, B.C. V6P 6E5

Published by Voyageur Press, Inc.
123 North Second Street, P.O. Box 338, Stillwater, MN 55082 U.S.A.
651-430-2210, fax 651-430-2211
books@voyageurpress.com
www.voyageurpress.com

Educators, fundraisers, premium and gift buyers, publicists, and marketing managers: Looking for creative products and new sales ideas? Voyageur Press books are available at special discounts when purchased in quantities, and special editions can be created to your specifications. For details contact the marketing department at 800-888-9653.

On page 1
Strawberry cactus blooms above the Rio Grande, Big Bend Ranch State Natural Area

On page 2
The Lighthouse formation rises abruptly from the floor of Palo Duro Canyon, Palo Duro Canyon State Park

On page 3
The afterglow of a sunset illuminates prairie grasses, Rita Blanca National Grasslands

On page 4
Morning sun gilds trees after rare autumn snowstorm, Enchanted Rock State Natural Area

On page 5
Sunrise at Onion Creek, McKinney Falls State Park, Texas Hill Country

On page 6
Bald cypress trees and Spanish moss at Mill Pond, Caddo Lake State Park, Texas Pineywoods

On page 7
Sand dunes cast in light of sunset, Padre Island National Seashore

On page 8
Sharp spines encircle a horse crippler cactus, Medina County

On page 9
Prickly pears and an abandoned house, Langtry, Texas

On page 10
Cirrus clouds streak across an inky blue sky above Rita Blanca National Grasslands

On page 11
Live oak tree and field of white prickly poppies and bluebonnets at sunset, Atascosa County

On the title page
The sun sets on a South Rim bluff, Big Bend National Park

Inset on the title page
Bluebonnets and Indian paintbrush, Washington County

DEDICATION

I dedicate this book to my grandson, Eliot Ransom Gordon Reynolds, whom I can't wait to show all the amazing places I've discovered in Texas.

ACKNOWLEDGMENTS

My sincere thanks go to all the dedicated personnel of the Texas Parks and Wildlife Department, the National Park Service, the National Wildlife Refuge System, and the National Forest Service, without whom we wouldn't have as many beautiful and special places in which to experience wild Texas. Thanks also to the Nature Conservancy of Texas, the Sierra Club, and the many other environmental organizations who work tirelessly to protect many other important wild areas of the state from being lost forever.

It was a pleasure to work with Michael Dregni of Voyageur Press, who suggested this project, and Kari Cornell, whose editing helped streamline the text and provide a focus for the presentation of my ideas.

Thanks also to Victor Emanuel, one of the strongest voices for conservation in Texas and a true friend of the environment, for graciously agreeing to write the foreword for this book.

My heartfelt thanks go out to my son, Ben, and daughter-in-law, Jessica, for accompanying me on those long hikes up to South Rim, helping me tote gear, and for just being there to experience the wonders of Big Bend with me.

Most importantly, I wish to thank my wife, Nancy, for her continued support, companionship, patience, and love through good times and bad.

Boulders and maple leaves,
Lost Maples State Natural Area

Contents

FOREWORD

by Victor Emanuel

Victor Emanuel holds a B.A. in zoology and botany from the University of Texas and an M.A. in government from Harvard University. In recognition of a lifetime of dedication to careful observation, education, and addition to the body of avian knowledge, Victor was the recipient of the 1993 Roger Tory Peterson Excellence in Birding Award, given by the Houston Audubon Society, the 2004 Roger Tory Peterson Award from the American Birding Association, and the 2004 Arthur A. Allen Award from the Cornell Laboratory of Ornithology. Victor is a member of the board of directors of the Cornell Laboratory of Ornithology.

THOSE WHO LOVE the natural world reserve a special place in their hearts for Texas. Except for the mountains of the Trans-Pecos, Texas lacks the dramatic scenery of places like Colorado, Utah, or Montana, but its biological diversity and richness exceed all other states. The Panhandle includes a portion of the Great Plains, while far to the south, the Neotropics reach their northern limit along the Rio Grande, the most biologically rich area in the world. The great forests of the southeastern United States reach their western limit in East Texas, while the mountains of the Sierra Madre of Mexico extend into the Big Bend Country. Central Texas is a unique area of limestone hills and clear streams. And the long Texas coast is one of the most exciting in the world for birdwatching. Each of the regions of Texas is worth a lifetime of visitation, study, and enjoyment.

Of the many marvelous natural phenomena that unfold in Texas every year, two deserve special mention: wildflowers and bird migration. The spring and early summer wildflower show in many parts of Texas is one of the wonders of the natural world. Even after many years, the Texas wildflower bloom still elicits the same sense of awe that it produced in me the first time I saw a field of bluebonnets, Indian paintbrush, or winecups.

I grew up in Houston and early in my life witnessed a fallout of migrating birds on the Texas coast. The scene remains etched in my memory: thousands of brightly colored migrating landbirds, having just flown across the Gulf of Mexico, had put down for a while in coastal woodlands. Seeing them was one of the most wonderful experiences of my life.

On the pages of *Wild Texas*, Richard Reynolds has captured some of the best scenery Texas has to offer. I hope this book will inspire those who open it to spend more time in the natural areas of Texas. They are a treasure. Although parts of Texas have been vastly altered over the past 200 years, much beauty remains for us to enjoy and protect.

A hazy sunset casts a warm glow over Enchanted Rock State Natural Area, Texas Hill Country

INTRODUCTION

Above
Boulders lie scattered in a field below El Capitan,
Guadalupe Mountains National Park

Left
A High Plains wheat field awaits harvesting,
Cochran County

Texas occupies a larger-than-life place in the minds of Texans and non-Texans alike. Those who have never been to Texas imagine a flat, endless expanse of cactus-covered desert. The Lone Star State does have a substantial amount of desert, but the land is far from flat and anything but lifeless. Yes, it is hot during the summer months, but anyone who has visited the majestic, forested mountains of Big Bend or the gentle, grassy slopes of the Davis Mountains in fall, winter, or spring can attest to the temperate, delightful weather that graces these areas most of the year. Those fortunate enough to have explored other regions within the state's 200,000 square miles have discovered verdant pine forests; sun-kissed, sandy beaches; clear, cypress-lined valley streams; wildflower-covered hills; and rolling prairies.

The state straddles four major physiographic regions: the Basin and Range province, the Great Plains, the Interior Lowlands, and the Gulf Coastal Plain. The Basin and Range province extends from central Nevada into western Texas, and consists of expansive desert drainage areas broken up by towering fault-block mountain ranges. The Davis Mountains, Big Bend National Park, and Guadalupe Mountains National Park are all found here.

In far northwestern Texas, the Great Plains extend into the state from the eastern base of the Rocky Mountains. This nearly flat, expansive region is broken up abruptly in the eastern panhandle by the Caprock escarpment, a rugged series of canyons created by the erosion of the high plains above.

The Interior Lowlands are the third major geological region. Extending from north-central Texas all the way to the Canadian border, this area includes the Rolling Plains, North Central Plains, Grand Prairie, and the Western and Eastern Cross Timbers. The Gulf Coastal Plain makes up the final region, which consists of the Blackland and Post Oak belts, the Coastal Prairie, the Pineywoods, the South Texas (or Rio Grande) Plains, and the Lower Rio Grande Valley.

The Lone Star State owes its varied landscape to a violent geological past. Evidence of massive volcanic eruptions, earthquakes, dramatic climate changes, and ancient seas that once covered much of the state has been uncovered in core samples taken during gas and oil exploration. Surface geological phenomena, such as the Capitan Reef in the Guadalupe Mountains, or Enchanted Rock, a billion-year-old Precambrian granite dome in the center of the state, also provide clues to the state's geological history. Similar ancient formations may also be found near Van Horn and El Paso in West Texas. These primeval rocks formed from cooling magma, and are sometimes referred to as the "basement complex"—rock that is believed to underlie not only the entire state of Texas, but all other continental masses as well.

The existence of other rocks such as shale, sandstone, and limestone, and fossils of animals similar to modern-day crustaceans such as brachiopods and snails

Freshly fallen snow covers the Chisos
Basin, Big Bend National Park

indicate that Texas was covered by shallow seas from the early Paleozoic era (350–600 million years ago) through the Cretaceous era (65–140 million years ago). During the early Cretaceous period, shallow seas deposited a layer of limestone eroded from nearby landforms and secreted by a variety of sea organisms on the sea floor. Because of subsequent uplifting processes, the limestone can be seen today in the towering walls of Santa Elena, Mariscal, and Boquillas canyons in Big Bend National Park, and in the canyons and headwaters of streams that drain the Edwards Plateau in West Central Texas.

Scientists believe the first humans arrived in Texas between 10,000 and 13,000 years ago. Little evidence remains of Texas's earliest settlers, though some tools and other artifacts have been found by archaeologists. Through the centuries, nature has worn down old settlements, and humans have not always been vigilant about protecting these sites from vandalism.

It is believed there were never more than 45,000 Native Americans in Texas at any time, and only a few thousand resided in Texas by the mid-nineteenth century. By the time the European explorers arrived in the sixteenth century, Texas was already a place where many Native American cultures mingled, traded, and fought one another. The influence of Spanish and French cultures had a major impact on the indigenous cultures, altering the trade networks, alliances, and demographics of the area. The distinct cultural identities of many groups were fractured through intermarriage and population loss. But the Spanish, despite their strong influence, were unable to conquer the Native Americans of Texas.

Because the Native Americans were able to secure goods and weapons from the French and later settlers in America, they remained relatively independent until the early nineteenth century. The Anglo-American migration into Texas changed the economic and political balance of the area, much to the detriment of the natives. The rapid influx of immigrants threatened their tribal hunting grounds and land bases. Unsuccessful attempts by Native Americans to keep the settlers' numbers in check only provoked retaliatory strikes. Eventually the natives were either killed or forced to leave the state.

Today there are only three reservations in Texas, and they are not populated with any of the tribes encountered by the Spanish and French explorers, rather with Native Americans who migrated to Texas after European colonization. The Alabama-Coushatta Reservation in East Texas near Livingston, the Tigua Reservation near El Paso, and the Kickapoo Reservation near Eagle Pass are all that remain of any organized Native American settlements in Texas.

Although Spanish explorers Cabeza de Vaca and Francisco Vasquez de Coronado each explored the region that would become the state of Texas, it was not until 1681, after the 1680 Pueblo Revolt in New Mexico, that the Spanish established the first permanent settlement in what is now El Paso. The Spaniards, who had been driven south from New Mexico by irate Pueblos, settled here, establishing the Ysleta and Socorro missions. The Spanish mission system was a frontier institution that sought to incorporate indigenous people into the Spanish colonial empire, converting them to Catholicism and immersing them in certain aspects of Spanish culture.

Four thousand-year-old pictograph,
Seminole Canyon State Park

French, English, German, Czech, Polish, and other European immigrants eventually settled in Texas as well. Their lasting influence may be seen today in towns like Fredericksburg (German), Panna Maria (Polish), and Fayetteville (Czech). What were these early explorers seeking? What prompted them to abandon their homelands, leaving behind familiar people, places, and cultures that had been established for hundreds of years? We can only guess what motivated these early Texas settlers to try to hack out an existence in the wild lands between the Red and Rio Grande rivers. Some no doubt came in pursuit of riches, others for freedoms they were unable to enjoy in their home countries, and yet others, perhaps, to simply start life anew.

Today, I can stand comfortably in the latest high-tech clothing and admire a stunning, snow-blanketed winter landscape in Big Bend National Park, knowing full well that I can retreat at any time to a warm, dry room or into my heated truck. From a comfortable frame of reference, it is much easier to admire the beauty and wonder of nature. Texas's earliest settlers climbed steep mountains not for the view, but to get to the other side of the mountain, perhaps in search of food, shelter, or water. Standing before a beautiful snowy landscape, were they able to appreciate the scenery for its aesthetic value, or did they see the snow as just another hardship?

There is no doubt that nature can be cruel. Interminable droughts, plagues of insects, and devastating windstorms all tax those who dare to take on Mother Nature. But while nature can be cruel, humans have returned the favor many times over, freely extracting what resources they need from the land for centuries without giving much thought to the consequences. Since the dawn of the Industrial Revolution, humans have discovered new ways to exact their will on nature, perhaps innocently at first, thinking that the air, water, and earth might endure one abuse after another.

What does it mean for land to be "wild"? *Merriam Webster's Collegiate Dictionary* defines it as "living in a state of nature" and "not amenable to human habitation." In 2001, a report released by the Governor's Task Force on Conservation determined that only about 2 percent of the state of Texas lies within a park, preserve, or wildlife management area. These are the places most people think of as "wild." More than 84 percent of the land in Texas is privately owned in the form of a ranch, farm, or forest. While most people do not think of farms and ranches as "wild," many rural land owners have for many years maintained their property in a mainly wild state and have allowed only a responsible amount of grazing by livestock. While much privately owned land can be considered wild, the abundance of wide open countryside gives many political leaders the idea that there is more wild land out there than really exists; hence, they feel no need to allocate money for conservation efforts. A pasture with grazing cattle might look wild, but it may or may not be managed in an environmentally responsible manner. An extreme example is the severe overgrazing in the early twentieth century, which transformed the land that is now Big Bend National Park from grassland to desert.

A joint study in 2003 by the American Farmland Trust and the Texas Cooperative Extension of Texas A&M University found that land fragmentation, which occurs when large- to mid-size ranches are divided into smaller "ranchettes," often results in significant changes in land use. While large ranches are most likely to remain native rangelands, the smaller, fragmented properties are more likely to be planted with nonnative species, leading to the loss of important wildlife habitats. Many ranch properties are being developed for recreational purposes, such as hunting, boating, and fishing, because these activities are much more profitable than agriculture.

The catch-22 of science and technology is that we adults, like small children discovering newfound abilities, seem to be unable to match our intellectual and technological abilities with the maturity to use them wisely. Our ultimate success as a civilization, and indeed our very survival, will depend on finding a way to manage the extravagant riches of planet Earth without in the process destroying the only home we've ever known.

Conservation of the wild lands we value requires the will and the effort of a majority of the people; we cannot rely only on the hard work of a few individuals or organizations. Preserving a cleaner environment for future generations will require a change in our perception of nature and in the way we go about nurturing and maintaining a fruitful and productive Earth. Conservation is an issue that affects everyone, regardless of political party, nationality, religion, or culture. Clean water and air are in everyone's best interest, and we need to make conservation a top priority.

This book represents part of the photographic record I have been making of Texas over the past three decades. In the process, I have learned many things about the state, have found places I hadn't dreamed existed, and have reveled in the simple pleasures of immersing myself in the wild. Human connectedness to the land is unmistakable: we came from the earth, we derive our sustenance from it, and we will, in the end, return to it.

I wish I could say that the pristine views in this book extended all around me, beyond the frame of each picture. In some cases (a very few) they did, but in most cases there were one or more human references in the landscape that I consciously made an effort to exclude: litter, road signs, discarded beer cans, or telephone poles, to name a few.

Cattle graze on the High Plains, Dallam County

Some photographers intentionally include such things to make a point—to show that humans have been here and left behind a record of their presence. However, my intent in presenting Texas as I have on these pages is not to fool anyone into thinking that everything out there is just fine or that these scenes are the rule rather than the exception. Nor do I want these photographs to serve merely as a visual record of wild Texas in the latter part of the twentieth century and the early part of the twenty-first century. Instead, I hope you will consider whether you think it's important for your children and grandchildren to be able to enjoy the beauty of Texas's wild places for years to come. If your answer is yes, then please do your part to help preserve the environment the next time you have the opportunity, whether by picking up a piece of trash someone else left behind, by recycling aluminum cans, or by voting for a candidate who will work to protect our wild lands for future generations.

Above all, I hope that this book will inspire people to go to a state or national park, to a preserve, or to a forest, and get out of the car, take a hike, smell a flower, take a photograph, or otherwise develop and sustain a relationship with nature. An enduring love for and respect of the environment will enrich your spirit, preserve your physical and emotional health, and lay the foundation for succeeding generations to do the same.

Chapter 1

EAST TEXAS PINEYWOODS

A PLACE OF SPLENDOR AND BIODIVERSITY

Above
An American alligator lurks just beneath the surface
Photo by John Elk III

Left
Bald cypress trees in autumn color at Mill Pond,
Caddo Lake State Park

Alligators were on my mind that morning. Not huge, man-eating crocodiles, mind you, but slithery, slinky green reptiles that glide through the swamp, threading their way between the moss-laden bald cypress trees, with just their dead eyes and bumpy backs protruding above the surface as they cruise the murky waters of Caddo Lake. Not that they would take a gastronomic interest in me if I were careless enough to fall out of my rented canoe, but I didn't want to test my luck.

Keep your balance, I muttered to myself, as I deliberately pulled one oar, then the other, through the duckweed, water lilies, and huge lotus pads, keeping an eye open for any reptiles, serpents, or otherwise muck-loving, mythical beasts that might inhabit the dark and mysterious waters beneath me. It would be just my luck, I thought, if some new species of Loch Ness–type monster decided to surface in Caddo Lake on the very day I find myself lost in the maze of canals, sloughs, swamps, and bayous that make up this strange but beautiful lake in northeastern Texas.

The morning was still and quiet, save for the occasional squawk of a bird, and I was thankful that the air was pleasantly cool. The last time I had ventured into this swamp was in the suffocating heat and humidity of July, when I'd come to photograph that queen of swamp wildflowers, the American lotus.

It was now late October, and I was trying to capture the brilliant orange tones of the bald cypress trees, the water-loving giants that shade the swamp. After a half-hour or so of determined paddling, I reached a grove of the trees in their best autumn finery. I had tried to photograph the trees on several previous attempts and failed. Timing is critical; the peak color in the swamp only stays around for a few days, and sudden windstorms have been known to blow all the leaves from the trees.

With nowhere to set a tripod in the murky waters of the swamp, I resorted to hand-held shooting. I had once tried to set up my tripod in the water, thinking the lake, which averages 4 feet in depth, was not as deep as my tripod was tall. The lake has a bottom all right, but it's not really a bottom. It's just several feet of thick, smelly, primordial goop that you don't want to disturb if you know what's good for you. My tripod was sucked right into the stuff.

Fortunately, I had brought my medium-format Pentax. It would allow me to get a good-sized transparency without having to use a tripod.

Holding my breath and being as still as one who is keeping an eye out for 'gators can be, I fired off a roll of film, bracketing my exposures, trying different focal lengths and angles. After fifteen minutes, feeling confident that I had gotten what I came for, I turned the canoe back around and began to paddle out of the swamp.

The East Texas Pineywoods region, a forested area that ranges from 75 to 125 miles wide and extends from the Red River south to within 25 miles of the Gulf

Cattle egret, Caddo Lake State Park

Bald cypress trees and ferns,
Caddo Lake State Park

Coast, was among the first regions to be settled in Texas, and its resources, most notably its timber, have been harvested for well over a hundred years. East Texas, with its gently rolling hills, ranges in elevation from only 200 to about 500 feet above sea level. The Pineywoods region is the most verdant in the state by virtue of its 40- to 60-inch annual rainfall totals and its acidic, sandy soils—ideal conditions for coniferous forests to take root.

Despite yielding many of its natural treasures to humans, East Texas remains a beautiful and unique part of the state. Forests of native loblolly and shortleaf pine are abundant, with hardwoods such as oak, magnolia, hickory, elm, gum, and tupelo mixed in, particularly in valleys and along rivers.

Before lumberjacks arrived, wielding heavy axes and sharp saws, longleaf pines also thrived in East Texas. Reaching heights of 100 feet or more, the longleaf pines sheltered an undergrowth of smaller trees, grasses, and wildflowers. By the middle of the twentieth century, however, only about 5 percent of the original longleaf forest remained, having been harvested nearly to exhaustion. The great trees were replaced by faster-growing pines or hardwoods, and today only isolated stands of longleaf pines can be found, primarily on preserves or in wetland savannas of the Big Thicket area in southeastern Texas.

The Big Thicket area is often referred to as a "biological crossroads" where swamps, hardwood forests, prairies, pine savannas, and dry sandhills meet and intermingle. Big Thicket National Preserve, which covers more than 97,000 acres within the Big Thicket area, was established October 11, 1974, to ensure the preservation, conservation, and protection of a portion of this once-great forest complex. Over thousands of years, natural processes have shaped an unlikely community of plants and animals within the preserve. Bald cypress swamps are found only a short distance from upland pine savannas and sandhills. Species of birds that normally do not frequent the same area, such as roadrunners and eastern bluebirds, may both be observed here. In 1981, the United Nations Education, Scientific and Cultural Organization (UNESCO) underscored the importance of this diverse ecosystem by designating it an International Biosphere Reserve.

An area as unusual as the Big Thicket, with as much history attached to it, is bound to be fodder for some tales of the weird. Many such stories stem from a ghostly light that purportedly appears at night on the old Bragg Road, an abandoned rail bed turned popular thoroughfare that runs through a dense wooded area of Big Thicket. In 1960, a local newspaper editor and environmentalist named Archer Fullingim, who influenced the creation of the Big Thicket National Preserve, ran a series of articles about the light. The articles were reprinted in newspapers across the country, attracting hordes of sightseers to the area. Many who have seen the light venture opinions about its nature and origin. Explanations range from the mundane—the light comes from car headlights, foxfire (a luminous fungus that causes decaying wood to glow), or swamp gas—to the fantastical—the light comes from a decapitated man searching for his head, which was severed from his body in a train wreck.

For a region that has seen so much urban and agricultural development over the years, it might be surprising to discover that there is still some wilderness left in East Texas. Without the efforts of the U.S. congressmen who pushed to pass the East Texas Wilderness Act of 1984, some of the last true wild lands in the region would have faced certain destruction at the hands of the logging industry. The act established and preserved five jewels of the region: Turkey Hill Wilderness Area, Indian Mounds Wilderness Area, Little Lake Creek Wilderness Area, Upland Island Wilderness Area, and Big Slough.

Situated within Angelina National Forest, Turkey Hill Wilderness Area encompasses 5,400 acres and nourishes a forest community of shortleaf and longleaf pine, pinewoods bluestem, southern red oak, white oak, and loblolly pine. Just 30 miles to the west, Indian Mounds Wilderness Area covers 12,000 acres and houses the largest remaining stand of threatened American beech and southern magnolia in the national forests of the United States. The rare and beautiful yellow lady's slipper orchid and broad beech fern can also be spotted at Indian Mounds.

Morning reflections in Mill Pond,
Caddo Lake State Park

Little Lake Creek Wilderness Area, a geologically young wilderness area comprising 4,000 acres, is found within Sam Houston National Forest. It is home to hawks, owls, and the endangered red-cockaded woodpecker, the latter of which can also be found at Upland Island Wilderness Area, the largest and most diversified wilderness area in East Texas. Upland Island, which covers 12,700 acres within Angelina National Forest, provides sanctuary for many threatened or endangered species, as well as some of the largest trees in the United States. The smallest of the five wilderness areas in East Texas is Big Slough, which encompasses 3,040 acres within Davy Crockett National Forest.

Other critical habitats in East Texas include the Caddo Lake area, in the heart of the Pineywoods region. Caddo Lake takes its name from "Kadohadacho," the name of a Native American tribe that inhabited the Red River country hundreds of years before the first European explorers arrived. Native American legend has it

Dogwood tree in bloom,
Sam Houston National Forest

that a long-ago Caddoan chief was warned by the Great Spirit to relocate his village to higher ground. He ignored the warning and a tremendous earthquake buried his village beneath what is now known as Caddo Lake.

While there was in fact a recorded earthquake and ensuing tremors in this region in the years 1811 and 1812, most scientists believe Caddo Lake was created over time by the formation of a massive 160-mile-long log-jam in the Red River. In 1874, the U.S. Army Corps of Engineers destroyed this log-jam, and by 1914, a real dam had been built near Mooringsport, Louisiana. In 1971, the U.S. Army Corps of Engineers tore down the old dam and constructed a new 1,540-foot earthen dam, Caddo Dam, which today serves a number of purposes, including water conservation and wildlife preservation.

Now contained by Caddo Dam, the 21,000-acre Caddo Lake extends from Caddo Parish, Louisiana, across the state line into Texas. It drains an area of more than 2,700 square miles and is popular among fisherman, boaters, birders, and nature lovers. In 1993, after blocking an attempt to construct a barge canal through the lake, environmentalists secured recognition of Caddo Lake as an international wetlands site, one of only seventeen such areas in the United States. It was awarded special recognition in part because of its biological diversity and the sanctuary it provides for migrating birds. Caddo Lake National Wildlife Refuge, established in 2000, protects more than 7,000 acres of old-growth hardwood forest along Harrison Bayou as well as the wetlands along Caddo Lake.

Despite efforts to save Caddo Lake and its habitats, there are still pressing problems that will affect its ultimate survival. Mercury and other heavy metals have been found in increasing amounts in the water and in many of the aquatic life

Above
Drummond phlox and spiderwort,
Cass County

Below
Coreopsis and sensitive briar,
Cass County

Above
Pitcher plants rise from a bog in Big
Thicket National Preserve

Left
Morning light in a cypress swamp,
Big Thicket National Preserve

forms that live here. In addition, would-be water barons, some of them former oil and gas marketers, are hoping to reap profits by selling the water from Caddo Lake to nearby cities in need. The lake is an unfortunate target in a marketing plan that would transform water into a precious commodity like oil in this region was in the early 1900s. Water development rights have been a hot-button issue across Texas for the past decade. How well we manage our water resources will determine whether Caddo Lake and other resources like it survive.

Right
Reflections in Turkey Creek, Big
Thicket National Preserve

Below
Young bald cypress trees grow in the
swamps of Martin Dies, Jr. State Park

Facing page
Giant blue iris, Bowie County

Early spring scene at Lake Daingerfield, Daingerfield State Park

Gilt-edged lily pads float on Lake Daingerfield

Above
Mushrooms sprout amidst autumn leaves, Tyler State Park

Left
Autumn color along Lake Daingerfield

Left
Sweetgum and bald cypress trees,
Big Cypress Creek

Below
Autumn colors at B. A. Steinhagen
Lake, Tyler County

Facing page
Sweetgum leaves cover the forest floor,
Atlanta State Park

Above
Chinese tallow, sweetgum, and maple trees shelter Ratcliff Lake, Davy Crockett National Forest

Facing page, top
Rare snowfall blankets Daingerfield State Park

Facing page, bottom
Winter scene at Daingerfield State Park

Chapter 2

TEXAS GULF COAST AND COASTAL PRAIRIES

IVORY BEACHES AND ROLLING DUNES

Above
A lone sand dollar awaits the next wave,
Padre Island National Seashore

Left
Sand dunes and beach flora,
Padre Island National Seashore

The Texas Gulf Coast region was the first part of the state seen by many early explorers. The first known European to sail into the Gulf was Sebastián de Ocampo, a Spanish explorer best known for circumnavigating Cuba in 1508. His discovery of the Gulf opened up a fresh route to the New World, and brought a host of new explorers. However, it was probably not until the 1519 voyage of Alonso Álvarez de Pineda—who explored the Gulf Coast from Florida to Cabo Rojo, Mexico—that any European laid eyes on the Texas mainland. Later Spanish explorers took a particular interest in the Texas barrier islands, which were at the time controlled by the Karankawa Indians, but the resistance of the Karankawa and the difficult geography of the region made it nearly impossible to open a port there.

The Texas coastline traces a jagged 624-mile-long line from tiny Boca Chica, Texas, where the Rio Grande joins the Gulf of Mexico, to the mouth of the Sabine River along the Louisiana border. Along the coast lie eight national wildlife refuges, one national seashore, and ten state parks. The Gulf Coast region encompasses more than just the crescent-shaped shoreline; it includes quiet salt marshes, rolling sand dunes, expansive tidal flats, and sprawling prairie wetlands.

Seven barrier islands—Galveston, Follets, Matagorda, San Jose (St. Joseph's), Mustang, Padre, and Brazos—extend along most of the Texas coastline, protecting the mainland from pounding waves and strong tides. Some of the islands are accessible only by boat, while others, such as Padre Island, are connected to the mainland by man-made bridges. The islands provide important habitat for both marine and terrestrial plants and animals, including a number of rare, threatened, and endangered species, such as the whooping crane, peregrine falcon, brown pelican, horned lizard, and Kemp's Ridley sea turtle. Since the islands are situated along the Central Flyway, they also provide much needed habitat for more than 350 migratory and resident species of birds.

I stand one early August morning on a stretch of Padre Island National Seashore, just a few yards from the water's edge, contemplating thousands of stars, a few brilliant planets, and the fuzzy glow of the Milky Way stretching from horizon to horizon. Having driven with two of my brothers 40 miles down the island from the prominent "4x4s ONLY" warning sign, I am far from civilization and its accompanying light pollution. The only other sites in Texas with skies this clear and black are in Big Bend Country.

The approach of dawn brings a faint glow of blue on the eastern horizon and the seagulls are airborne again, cruising over our campsite in search of handouts. I'm standing with my camera just a few feet from the crashing surf, hoping for a spectacular sunrise. The azure sky gradually gives way to pale blue, and then tones of crimson, magenta, and gold paint the wispy cirrus clouds as sunrise approaches. There is only sky and water before me—no wildflower fields, no mountains, no canyons, no high plains vistas. I'm here to capture pure light—reflected from the heavens, bounced off the water and into my lens.

Facing page
Morning sunlight reflects in surf at
Padre Island National Seashore,
Kleberg County

I wish I could freeze time, so I wouldn't have to constantly recalculate my exposures as light levels change. Wishes aside, between strong gusts of wind I make my exposures, trying to minimize the effects of vibration. Before I know it, the sun is up, the moment has passed, and my sunrise photography session is over.

After dropping off my gear at my campsite, I trudge up a nearby sand dune to see the island from a higher perspective. Padre Island spans 70 miles from north to south, the longest barrier island in the world. The shoreline stretches in both directions as far as my eyes can see; to the east, unusually clear and beautiful blue-green water greets me, while to the west, sand dunes and coastal prairie extend to the Laguna Madre, some 2 miles distant.

Five thousand years from now, this view will probably be startlingly different. The waterlines, sand dunes, grasslands, and tidal flats of Padre Island are constantly being reshaped by the relentless forces of wind and water. Its beaches are composed of fine white sand, and range from a few dozen to several hundred feet wide. Along the far edge of the beaches, running parallel to the shoreline, are ridges of sand dunes formed by blowing sand. Powerful hurricanes, such as Bret in 1999, Allen in 1980, and Beulah in 1967, can cut gaps through these dune ridges, allowing sand to escape. The escaped sands gather in new "blowout" dunes, which eventually stabilize and sometimes form very large dune fields.

Padre Island National Seashore is home to many endangered sea turtles and is one of the only sites in the world tourists can visit to view sea turtle hatchlings being released into the wild. A multi-agency program is underway there to increase sea turtle nesting, including the Kemp's Ridley, the most endangered sea turtle in the world. Beginning in late spring and continuing through the summer months, patrolling volunteers and staff search for nests, and biologists collect sea turtle eggs to be cared for at the park's incubation facility. After hatching, the sea turtles are released into the Gulf. By monitoring the hatch and release, biologists help prevent birds, coyotes, and other opportunistic animals from gobbling up the sea turtles before they can make the short journey from their nests to the water.

Farther up the coastline, past Padre, Mustang, and San Jose islands, visitors will discover Aransas National Wildlife Refuge, which was established in 1937. Its 70,504 acres are comprised of grasslands, oak mottes, and redbay thickets that thrive in deep, sandy soils. Wildlife found in this refuge include deer, javelina, coyote, bobcat, and more than 392 species of birds, but the rare and endangered whooping crane is the most famous species at Aransas. During the late fall, winter, and early spring months, the cranes eat the clams and crabs that live in the tidal flats. Whooping cranes weren't always as plentiful as they are now. In 1941, there were only fifteen in the refuge. By late 2003, after years of intense conservation efforts, whooping crane numbers had increased to around 200. Visitors can usually see the cranes from the refuge's observation tower from late October through mid April.

Clockwise, from upper left
Quahog shell fragments, Padre Island National Seashore

Quahong seashells on the beach, South Padre Island

Coquinas, scallops, and shell fragments, Padre Island National Seashore

Scallops, starfish, and assorted seashells, Mustang Island State Park

Big Boggy, San Bernard, and Brazoria national wildlife refuges lie in a cluster along the central Texas Gulf Coast. Like Aransas, these refuges provide sanctuary for hundreds of bird species. Their coastal wetlands provide critical habitat for both waterfowl and migratory songbirds. They are also a popular destination for travelers seeking escape from the nearby city of Houston, which lies to the northeast.

Southeast of Houston, Anahuac National Wildlife Refuge borders Galveston Bay; the refuge consists of bayous, coastal prairies, and bogs. Songbirds are a common sight here in the spring and fall, and roseate spoonbills, egrets, white-faced ibis, and mottled ducks are year-round denizens. Tens of thousands of snow geese and dozens of duck species overwinter in the park's wetland areas. Visitors may even catch a glimpse of an endangered red wolf.

Unfortunately, years of illegal offshore dumping combined with accidental oil or hazardous waste spills have polluted the Gulf waters and have deposited trash on the once-pristine Gulf beaches. While some areas of the coast, like those within Padre Island National Seashore and the national wildlife refuges, have been put under federal protection, many other miles of shoreline have seen extensive development. Increased development along the coast means there are fewer areas where the millions of migrating birds can land and roost. As of 2005, the Texas Gulf Coast region had well over 5 million residents, and pressures on the natural resources of the area continue to grow. The early Spanish navigators would hardly recognize the area today.

As my brothers and I leave the far reaches of Padre Island National Seashore, I take one last look at the crashing surf, the wind-sculpted sand dunes held in place by golden sea oats and sprawling railroad vine, and the flocks of brown pelicans flying only a few inches above the water. I leave with a newfound appreciation and respect for the natural forces that built this special place, and I feel grateful that I was able to spend a few days on this jewel of the Texas coast.

Above
Dusk reflections in surf,
Chambers County

Below
Seagulls at sunrise,
Padre Island National Seashore

Sunrise paints sky and surf, Padre Island National Seashore, Kleberg County

Right
Endangered Kemp's Ridley sea turtle
hatchlings race for the waves.
Photograph © Doug Perrine /
SeaPics.com

Below
Patterns in the sand,
Padre Island National Seashore

Above
Sea oats bend in a strong gulf breeze, Padre Island National Seashore

Right, top
Goat's-foot morning glories cascade down a sand dune,
Padre Island National Seashore

Right, bottom
A solitary beach morning glory grows through fallen sea oats,
Padre Island National Seashore

Above
Live oak tree, Goose Island State Park

Left
Wind-swept oak trees shelter Goose Island State Park

Above
Coastal prairie vista, San Bernard National Wildlife Refuge

Facing page, left
Giant blue irises in bloom, Anahuac National Wildlife Refuge

Facing page, right
Mixed coastal prairie flora, San Bernard National Wildlife Refuge

Chapter 3

HILL COUNTRY AND EDWARDS PLATEAU

LAND OF CLEAR SPRINGS AND EMERALD HILLS

Above
Flowers and gneiss boulders at Valley Spring,
Inks Lake State Park

Left
Limestone formations along the Pedernales
River, Pedernales Falls State Park

A T THE GEOGRAPHICAL center of Texas, between the Pecos and Colorado rivers, lies a region of juniper-studded hills, steep canyons, clear valley streams lined with huge bald cypress and pecan trees, fields bursting with wildflowers, and abundant wildlife. Known simply as the Texas Hill Country, this area occupies a large portion of the Edwards Plateau, the southernmost unit of the Great Plains. Some folks claim the Hill Country is a state of mind. That may well be, but for me it's a place, and a darn good one at that.

I grew up in San Antonio, which is at the crossroads of three of the seven distinct geographical regions described in this book: South Texas Brush Country, Blackland Prairie, and Hill Country. As kids, my brothers and I spent a substantial amount of our free time hanging out in the more or less Brush Country habitat of San Antonio's west side. Mesquite trees, yuccas, and prickly pear were common near our home. My family also owned land near Hondo—40 miles to the southwest—that was most definitely considered Brush Country. We chased many an armadillo through the thorny blackbrush and guajillo scrub, collected spiky horny toads and lumbering Berlandier's tortoises, and hunted our share of rattlesnakes and cottontails on that property, which to this day, I'm proud to say, is pretty much the way it was back then.

We also explored the Hill Country, the southernmost edge of which brushes up against the northwest side of San Antonio. In the early 1950s, development in San Antonio barely extended out from Loop 410, which encircles the city. Our father took us on frequent day trips to places like Helotes, Kerrville, and Fredericksburg, which at the time seemed like utopia. In fact, someone decided to name a Hill Country town Utopia some years back, and while the cypress-lined Sabinal River bottomland that graces that town is indeed utopia, the qualities that make it so extend well beyond its city limits.

My father took us to the best swimming holes, the coolest balanced rocks, the most spectacular overlooks, and the best fishing spots in the Hill Country. He introduced us to Enchanted Rock, the most awesome geological structure in the state, which was then a privately owned ranch and is now a state park. He acquainted us with the glories of the Guadalupe River, where we swam and played for hours on end while he made his business calls in Kerrville.

The necessities of going to school and cultivating a social life kept me away from the Hill Country during my high school and college years. I did not return until my early thirties, when I landed a job as photographer for the Texas Tourist Development Agency—the government entity blessed with the task of enticing those unfortunate enough not to live in Texas to at least visit the Lone Star State and leave their money there. My business trips to the Hill Country during those years reacquainted me with its many charms, and I discovered plenty of new charms too. My further explorations of this gem of a place were enhanced by the acquisition of a small body of knowledge of the area, which I try to add to on a somewhat intermittent basis.

The Texas Hill Country lies on the Edwards Plateau, a region of about 17 million acres in Central Texas. The Balcones Fault, a great crack in the earth that separates the Rocky Mountain uplands from the coastal lowlands, forms the southern and eastern borders of the Edwards Plateau, while the Rolling Plains define the northern boundary, and the Pecos-Devils River divide creates the western boundary. Elevations on the Edwards Plateau range from about 100 feet to over 3,000 feet. The southern and western third of the plateau is heavily dissected by deep, lush river valleys that harbor oak forests, Ashe-juniper and oak woodlands, and, in some protected areas of the canyons, rare colonies of bigtooth maple trees.

As in many other areas of the state, a long history of overgrazing has led to a significant reduction in the grasslands in this region. Little bluestem, Texas cup grass, cane bluestem, and sideoats grama (the official state grass) were once dominant in the open woodlands, with scattered mottes of live-oak and cedar-elm trees thriving in the once deep soil. Today, Texas grama, three-awns, and hairy tridens have replaced the dominant grasses, and the tree and shrub population, including live oak, mesquite, Ashe juniper, and agarita, have replaced grass in many areas where humans have suppressed naturally occurring wildfires and have allowed cattle to overgraze.

E. H. Johnson, at the *Handbook of Texas Online* (www. tsha.utexas.edu), describes the Edwards Plateau as "an erosional region with thin soil over beveled Comanchean limestone." What this implies, Johnson continues, is that "if any such loose soil ever mantled the Edwards Plateau, it has long since been carried away by erosion." A visit to most areas in the region will bear this out: there's not much topsoil covering the limestone. What soil hasn't made it to the Gulf of Mexico yet has settled in lower elevations such as river bottoms. Huge pecan trees and bald cypresses have taken root in this rich soil along the banks of most Hill Country rivers—the Guadalupe, Sabinal, Medina, Frio, Llano, Pedernales, Nueces, and Colorado.

Anyone who has lived in or spent much time visiting the Hill Country might wonder where all the limestone came from. Between 65 and 140 million years ago, during the period known as the Cretaceous era (*creta* is the Latin word for chalk), shallow, relatively calm seas covered North America. A motley assortment of gastropods, echinoids, ammonites, and a few large, swimming dinosaurs, such as the mosasaurus, made their home in this sea. The waters of the sea eventually receded, leaving behind fossils of these creatures in the limestone beds, and a substantial industry has been created to mine this fossilized stone for architectural use.

Fog settles over the hills in Bandera County

Morning light reveals a pastoral scene in Bandera County

A geological anomaly exists in the middle of the Hill Country, commonly called the Central Mineral Region or Llano Uplift. This area is known for its abundance and diversity of minerals unequaled in the state: quartz, granite, gneiss, flint, schist, feldspar, and limestone. The granite highlands in northern Gillespie, Llano, and Burnet counties cover about 3,000 square miles. Enchanted Rock, which straddles the Gillespie-Llano county line, is the focal point of the region. Like a great iceberg at sea that hides most of its mass underwater, the main granite dome is only a portion of the massive Enchanted Rock batholith, which extends underground across a hundred-square-mile area. Robert M. Reed, at his website *Rob's Granite Page* (uts.cc.utexas.edu/~rmr), defines a batholith as "a large granitic body made up of multiple intrusions of igneous [volcanic] rock." The dome of Enchanted Rock rises 425 feet above the surrounding land. It is believed to be more than 1 billion years old, ranking it among some of the oldest rocks on Earth.

As with other natural oddities, Enchanted Rock has been the source of a number of colorful stories over the years. The Tonkawa Indians, who lived in the area hundreds of years ago, reported seeing ghost fires on the dome and hearing odd sounds emanating from the rock. They attributed these phenomena to spiritual and mystical forces, but scientists commonly believe the incessant cycle of heating and cooling the dome undergoes during the hot summer months is what creates the eerie sounds.

Another legend recounts the tale of a Spaniard imprisoned by the Tonkawa. The prisoner escaped and hid among the scattered rocks and boulders, but to the Tonkawa it appeared as though he had been swallowed by the great rock. Legends grew from the event, relating that the man swallowed by the rock was responsible for casting spells on the area.

Inks Lake State Park, one of the most beautiful spots in the Hill Country, also lies within the Llano Uplift. It is one of seven lakes on the Highland Lakes chain of the Colorado River. Its crystal-clear blue waters are popular with boaters, fishermen, divers, and swimmers. Pink granite boulders and outcroppings are scattered throughout the oak and juniper woodlands that surround the lake.

In spring, masses of bluebonnets, sprinkled with spiderwort, Drummond's phlox, Indian paintbrush, and coreopsis, bloom among the boulder fields and along the rocky slopes above Inks Lake. Birders come from all over to see ospreys, red-breasted mergansers, common loons, vireos, warblers, and the rainbow-hued painted bunting. Only a few miles away along the upper reaches of Lake Buchanan, bald eagles come to roost from mid November through mid March, drawing a good number of ogling tourists.

Birders come to the Hill Country especially to see two endangered species: the golden-cheeked warbler, which nests in the verdant canyons of the Edwards Plateau, and the black-capped vireo, which nests in scrubby thickets on the dry slopes and rocky uplands of the region. The Texas Parks and Wildlife website (www.tpwd.state.us) reports that "of the nearly 360 bird species that breed in Texas, the golden-cheeked warbler is the only one that nests exclusively in Texas." The warblers travel great distances during their migration between Texas and Mexico or Central America, arriving in Texas in March to nest and raise their young in sheltered habitats forested with oak and juniper trees, and leaving in July to winter in Mexico and Central America. Golden-cheeked warblers are endangered because so many of the forests they need to survive have been cut down to make way for housing developments, road construction, and agricultural purposes, while other habitats have been flooded behind dams.

Destruction of habitat has also had a critical impact on the black-capped vireo. These tiny birds nest in Texas from April through July, and overwinter in Mexico. Vireos build nests in low-growing shrubbery, a habitat which, like that of the golden-cheeked warbler, is slowly disappearing.

Ask any number of people what they love about the Texas Hill Country and they will tell you it is the legendary bluebonnets, millions upon millions of them carpeting pastures, fields, hillsides, roadsides, front yards, riverbanks, and any other area with a few square feet of available space. A story is told that the first explorers to come to the Texas Hill Country gazed upon mile after mile of the cerulean blue and white blossoms, covering hillsides as far as the eye could see. I suspect there might be an ounce of exaggeration in that tale, but it's not too hard to believe if you happen to be here in March or April of a good wildflower year.

To some, the bluebonnet hysteria is nauseating. There are bluebonnet festivals, bluebonnet trails, bluebonnet paintings, bluebonnet photos, bluebonnet T-shirts, and so on. Texans love their bluebonnets and they treasure photographs of the popular flower. I confess to having recorded a bluebonnet or two on film over the years. Of course, I don't mind if there are a few other species of flowers growing among the bluebonnets: scarlet Indian paintbrush, pink Drummond phlox, or red and yellow gaillardia, to name a few.

The bluebonnet (or lupine) is the official state flower of Texas. There are actually five species of them, all considered the state flower. *Lupinus texensis* is the most common bluebonnet, the one you see in the Hill Country and the flower most often depicted in paintings and photographs. It peaks between late March and mid April. *Lupinus subcarnosus,* the sandy-land bluebonnet, grows in Leon, LaSalle, and parts of Hidalgo counties. It prefers sandy soils and its blooms peak in late March.

The most majestic of the bluebonnets is *Lupinus havardii,* also known as the Big Bend bluebonnet; it frequently reaches 3 feet in height. *Lupinus havardii* grows in washes and arroyos, on rocky limestone slopes, and along roadsides in Big Bend National Park and the surrounding areas, sometimes blooming as early as January and lasting through April. It is particularly spectacular when golden desert marigolds bloom alongside it. The remaining two bluebonnets are *Lupinus concinnus,* native to West Texas and the runt of the group, reaching only 7 inches in height; and *Lupinus plattensis*, a denizen of the Texas Panhandle that grows to about 2 feet tall and is the only perennial of the group.

Many who have visited the Texas Hill Country have been enchanted by its beauty and have waxed poetic about its charms. Perhaps William Bollaert, the English traveler and adventurer who explored Texas in the 1840s, said it best in his book *William Bollaert's Texas* (originally published in 1843):

Facing page
Gaillardia, bluebonnets, lazy daisies, and spotted bee balm bloom in McCulloch County

It is difficult to give a full and just description of this spot with its surrounding scenery. If Rome was celebrated in song for her "seven hills," Austin may well boast of her "thousand mounds," covered with bowers equal in splendor to the Arcadian groves. The native beauty of the Colorado is not surpassed by any part of North America. Its mountains, its vales, its hills and its dales are ever before the eye, and when we tire of gazing upon the one we can turn with delight to the other. Every shade of the majestic and beautiful can be traced in the wide prospect, where the brightest and sunniest spots slope gently to those of shady luxuriance . . . where the blossoms open "mid darkness and gloom," while the sun of heaven smiles brightly on the land below.

Right
Maple leaves adorn a mullein plant,
Lost Maples State Natural Area

Below
Fall color brightens the banks of the
Sabinal River, Lost Maples State
Natural Area

Facing page
Bigtooth maple trees in autumn splendor, Lost Maples State Natural Area

Above, top
Stately bald cypress trees take root along
the placid Frio River in Uvalde County

Above, bottom
Bald cypress trees line the banks of the
Guadalupe River, Kerr County

Left
Trees line this rapid-laden stretch of the
Guadalupe River near Gruene

Above
Water cascades over the upper falls,
Pedernales Falls State Park

Right
Sunrise gilds trees at Onion Creek,
McKinney Falls State Park

Left
White-tailed deer, Inks Lake State Park

Below
Possumhaw trees provides vivid color
along Barton Creek, Travis County

Ashe juniper and possumhaw trees, Barton Creek Greenbelt

Above
A nearly full moon glows above
Enchanted Rock, Enchanted Rock
State Natural Area

Left
Cirrus clouds and granite boulder,
Enchanted Rock State Natural Area

Flowers and gneiss boulders
at Valley Spring, Inks Lake
State Park

Left
Prickly pear buds, Kerr County

Below
Prickly pears glow at sunset in a Kerr County field

Above, left
Coreopsis, gaillardia, horsemint, and peppergrass, San Saba County

Above, right
Prairie paintbrush and bluebonnets bloom in McCulloch County

Facing page
Bluebonnets, Indian paintbrush and bladderpod, Mason County

Chapter 4

PANHANDLE PLAINS

BIG BLUE SKIES AND
BURNT ORANGE CANYONS

Above
Buffalo gourd, gaillardia, and woolly
paperflower, Palo Duro Canyon

Left
A bare juniper tree stands on the slopes of
Capitol Mesa, Palo Duro Canyon State Park

THE GREAT AMERICAN artist Georgia O'Keeffe taught art in Amarillo, Texas, from 1912 to 1913, back when it was just a dusty, windy town on the High Plains of Texas. O'Keeffe, ever the inventive and perceptive artist, reacted strongly but positively to the qualities of this seemingly bleak land, incorporating many of its elements into her later paintings of the American Southwest: the broad cobalt skies; the burnt orange canyons, hills, and rocks; the ruddy rivers; the ochre dust that seems to cling to everything; even the bleached animal bones that lie scattered across the prairie.

In 1916, after spending time in New York, Virginia, and South Carolina, O'Keeffe returned to Texas to accept a job at West Texas State Normal College (now West Texas A&M University) in Canyon. At this time, she set aside her customary charcoals and began using vibrant oils and watercolors. The essence of the Texas Panhandle had been permanently burned into her consciousness, and elements of it appeared in her work for the rest of her long and productive life.

O'Keeffe's reaction to the high plains and rolling prairies of northwestern Texas is one ultimately felt by many people who spend time in this part of the state. The Texas Panhandle, with its sprawling, pancake-flat plains and deeply incised canyons, has been described as a mountain range turned upside down.

Wedged in between Oklahoma to the north and east, and New Mexico to the west, the boundaries of the Texas Panhandle were determined by the Compromise of 1850, which settled border disputes between Texas and its neighboring states. Originally 50 percent larger than its current size, the Panhandle now covers 25,610 square miles and is dominated by the High Plains, while the Rolling Plains making up a small portion of the southeast. The region consists primarily of vast, open

Right
A wet spring creates a verdant landscape at Palo Duro Canyon State Park

Facing page, top
An ominous thunderhead grows on the distant horizon, Palo Duro Canyon State Park

Facing page, bottom
A rainbow signals the passing of another spring thunderstorm, Palo Duro Canyon State Park

grasslands, with tree growth having been hampered by low humidity and periodic, naturally occurring fires. Once home to large herds of buffalo, the area was later overtaken by ranchers and their cattle, and today supports an agriculture-based economy.

The High Plains were created when rock and sediment debris from the formation of the Rocky Mountains traveled eastward by way of rivers and streams to be deposited on the area where the High Plains now sit. Lime (calcium carbonate) was also carried to the High Plains by run-off from the mountains, entering the soil and forming layers of caliche (a cementlike sediment), often found today beneath layers of sand or soil.

The Canadian River cuts across the High Plains to isolate the southern part of the Panhandle, a plateau known as the Llano Estacado (variously translated as "staked plain" or "palisaded plain"), which is one of the world's flattest areas of such size. The Llano Estacado covers approximately 32,000 square miles and is roughly bounded by the Canadian River valley, the Caprock escarpment, the Mescalero escarpment of New Mexico, and the Johnson Creek branch of the Colorado River.

The origin of the term "Llano Estacado" is uncertain. There are many historical references to "stakes" used as a way to navigate through the broad plains; for example, stakes were used to mark routes through the plains. However, it's perhaps more likely the name is derived from the geological features of the area, the steep escarpments or bluffs found along the eastern, northern, and western boundaries of the area that were often referred to by early explorers as "palisades" or "ramparts." Some historians believe the Llano Estacado was named by Spanish explorer Francisco Vázquez de Coronado in 1541, upon his sighting of the most famous escarpment of the area, the Caprock escarpment, which forms the eastern border of Llano Estacado.

The Caprock escarpment, a spectacular 300-foot-high cliff carved by erosion, separates the High Plains from the more humid lower plains to the east. The caprock itself is not a rock layer in the usual sense of the term, but is more technically a "hard-pan" layer of mostly mineral subsoil particles that have cemented themselves together to form a rocklike layer a few feet below the ground (caliche). The land is one of colorful cliffs and canyons and abundant wildlife, including African aoudad sheep, whitetail and mule deer, pronghorns, golden eagles, raccoons, coyotes, bobcats, opossums, porcupines, foxes, and more than 175 species of birds.

It has taken some 90 million years for nature to carve, slice, and erode Palo Duro Canyon into a portion of the Caprock escarpment. The canyon is up to 800 feet deep, stretches 120 miles long, and reaches widths of up to 20 miles across; it is sometimes called the second-biggest canyon in the United States—second to the Grand Canyon, of course.

Above
Winter vista along the Prairie Dog Town Fork of the Red River, Palo Duro Canyon State Park

Facing page
The lower slopes of Capitol Mesa glow in afternoon sunlight, Palo Duro Canyon State Park

Above, top
Receding storm clouds, Palo Duro
Canyon State Park

Above, bottom
The sun sets on a snow-dusted landscape, Palo Duro Canyon State Park

Facing page
Canyon vista after a winter storm,
Caprock Canyons State Park

Rainbow-colored layers in fan-shaped formations within the canyon are sometimes referred to as "Spanish skirts." Pinnacles, buttes, knobs, hoodoos, and mesas jut out from the bottom and sides of the gorge. Scientists and hobbyists alike have uncovered numerous fossils in the rock layers, which span across 240 million years in age. In years with adequate winter and spring rains, spectacular wildflower displays fill the canyon, to the delight of visitors.

On a late June day several years ago, after a very wet winter and spring, I traveled 500 miles from Austin to Palo Duro Canyon State Park. The flowers that lined the roads and filled the fields along the way were a sneak preview of the extravagance to come. Horsemint, gaillardia, and woolly paperflower formed nearly impenetrable waist-high colonies on the floor of the canyon; impenetrable not just because of their superlative growth, but also because of the abundance of thirsty mosquitoes roosting in colonies so dense that I'd swear they were causing the poor plants to lean over from all the extra weight. This is, of course, the downside to all the life-giving rain: it also gives life to blood-sucking insects.

Trying to ignore the hordes of treacherous mosquitoes, I plodded ahead to get my photos. Female mosquitoes are the ones that pierce the skin. Their mouthparts form a long, sucking proboscis. Males have feathery antennae and their mouthparts are not suitable for penetrating the skin. A mosquito's principal food is nectar, and here that source was, growing right in front of me; I was determined to photograph it.

The field of yellow, magenta, red, and pink flowers created a stunning foreground for my composition. The background was none other than Capitol Peak, the most prominent landmark in the park. I had arrived at the site a good half-hour before sunrise to set up my tripod, camera, lens, and any necessary accessories. The mosquitoes, delighted to see me, descended upon my body, ignoring foul-smelling repellent and thick clothing as they burrowed their wretched snouts into my skin. But I worked, waving my arms about wildly to fend off the little beasts that were intent on having me for breakfast.

The sun finally rose high enough over the mesa behind me to light distant Capitol Peak but still leave me in shadow. A split-density gray filter would bring the light level on the distant horizon in line with that of the foreground. I made several exposures, furiously blowing and waving the flying attackers away from the lens, all the while trying to keep them from getting inside the camera and making shadowgrams of their puny little bodies on my film.

I managed to come away with some nice images, despite my run-in with the kamikaze insects. The mosquitoes were only a factor in temporarily altering my vocabulary and body topography, and did not spoil any of the exposures I made that day. I wondered, as I left the canyon with many new welts on my face and neck, if Georgia O'Keeffe had had any encounters with of the dastardly blood-suckers of the canyon, and if so, did it influence her love for the place? Probably not.

Above
Light of sunset highlights ridges at
Caprock Canyons State Park

Left
A collared lizard basks in the sun in
Caprock Canyons State Park

Far left
Yuccas grow on canyon rim, Caprock
Canyons State Park

Sunflowers bloom in a Briscoe County field

Yuccas and a mesquite tree grow above Mackenzie Reservoir, Briscoe County

Facing page, top left
Basketflowers fill a Dickens County field

Facing page, top right
A prairie dog surveys his territory at Mackenzie State Park in Lubbock

Below, left
Sunset over sky and grasslands, Hutchinson County

Below
Horsemint, Mexican hats, and woolly paperflowers punctuate the
High Plains landscape, Motley County

Left
Grasses glow at sunrise
in Rita Blanca National
Grasslands

Below
Old windmill and cattle
pens, Rita Blanca
National Grasslands

Facing page
Grasslands in autumn,
Rita Blanca National
Grasslands

Chapter 5

SOUTH TEXAS PLAINS

BEAUTIFUL BRUSH COUNTRY

Above
Prickly pear with ripe tunas, Zavala County

Left
Rose prickly poppies and sunflowers bloom
amidst prickly pears, La Salle County

It's a chilly November morning and I'm trying to pry myself from my down sleeping bag before sunrise. The initial shock of moving from the cozy comfort of my sleeping bag to near-freezing temperatures makes me think twice about getting up. Being a landscape photographer, however, I have an unspoken professional duty to be up and ready to shoot at the crack of dawn, to take advantage of some of the best light of the day.

I'm finally up, scrambling to find my gloves and parka before frostbite claims any of my exposed extremities. I make a quick cup of steaming coffee, which fogs my glasses as I stare blankly into it, wondering what I'm doing here in this freezing weather. I remember I'm here to take a picture. Then up a frozen aluminum ladder I climb, tripod and camera in one hand and a bag slung over my shoulder, in search of a strategic vantage point from the roof of my South Texas cabin.

Some would say I'm cheating by taking a picture from the roof of a house. I imagine the purists would demand that I shinny up a mesquite tree if I need to shoot from any altitude higher than eye level. Fact is, when you're in the South Texas thornscrub, you're usually on fairly flat land with very few trees. Elevated vistas are at a premium, and there never seems to be one when and where you need it.

I set up my camera and wait. Minutes pass as the light of day begins to reveal the landscape below me. My family's cabin sits on a small hill overlooking a broad sweep of classic South Texas Brush Country. Small shrubs such as guajillo, blackbrush, and cenizo make up about 80 percent of the vegetation here, while Texas persimmon, live oak, spiny hackberry, and the ubiquitous mesquite tree make up the majority of the tree population. At this time of the year, most of the shrubs have already dropped their leaves, but the mesquites are stubbornly hanging onto theirs. A blanket of fog weaves in and out of the trees as dawn approaches. The naked, black limbs of dead and dormant trees scattered throughout the woods below me seem to be reaching upward through the fog, as though they might find renewed life on the other side.

Sandhill cranes fly in flocks of from two to thirty birds. Their unmistakable calls pierce the frigid morning air; otherwise, it is so quiet you can hear them coming from at least a mile away. Cottontail rabbits and field mice are busy doing something below me, and in the distance a cow bellows as if to register her disapproval with the freezing temperatures.

A tiny magenta arc of the sun suddenly slips above an oak motte in the distance. Layers of red, orange, pink, and yellow, due to droplets of water and particles of God-knows-what in the atmosphere, lend a painterly quality to the scene. I am at once cursing the air pollution and reveling in its fantastic photographic properties. Knowing the sky is four to eight times brighter than the foreground, I position a split-density gray filter over the lens to balance the exposure.

The South Texas Plains are roughly bounded to the west by the Rio Grande, to the north by Highway 90 between Del Rio and San Antonio, and to the east by an irregular border running from San Antonio to Goliad, then south to Browns-

Left
Pink evening primrose and prairie
verbena blooms along a roadside in
Frio County

Facing page, top
Guajillo leaves form a lacy tapestry,
Medina County

Facing page, bottom
Mountain laurel, guajillo, and cenizo,
Medina County

ville. The region, part of the Tamaulipan Biotic Province (most of which lies in Mexico), exhibits a great variety of landforms, soils, vegetation, and wildlife. The Lower Rio Grande Valley is home to plant and bird species found nowhere else in the United States. The subtropical Chihuahuan Thorn Forest is also unique within in the United States. If you can get beyond the assorted stickers, barbs, burrs, and needles (admittedly no small task), it's easy to take a liking to this underappreciated part of the state.

The diversity of the plants and animals living in the Brush Country is astounding. This area is home to many tropical species that abound in Mexico, several grassland species that range northward, and some desert species commonly found in the Trans-Pecos. In wet years, I spend more time photographing wildflowers here than I do in other areas of the state. They often begin blooming in late February and continue into June. Cacti are particularly plentiful here, and you can find them blooming in more colors than in most other regions of the state.

The South Texas Plains receive between 20 and 32 inches of precipitation annually, classifying them as subhumid to dry. The region receives most of its annual precipitation from sea breezes and air mass thunderstorms, which roll in from the Gulf of Mexico nearly every day during summer months, and from occasional tropical storms and hurricanes.

Above, top
Indian paintbrush, bluebonnets, primroses, prickly poppies, and Huisache trees bloom in a Karnes County field

Above, bottom
Gaillardia, bluebonnets, and Engelmann's daisies, Frio County

The South Texas vegetation has probably changed little through the centuries, consisting of shrubs and grasslands altered only by the amount of moisture received in any given year. Some of the first written reports of vegetation in the area, stemming from the 1600s, describe extensive grasslands and large thickets of trees and shrubs.

When ranchers began to keep livestock on these plains in the early nineteenth century, overgrazing led to diminished grasslands and an increase in brush cover, trends which increased into the twentieth century. Ranchers employed various methods to control the growth of brush, but in the late 1960s, biologists discovered that extensive brush removal harmed wildlife and they thus discouraged ranchers from employing it. As a result, wildlife populations, most notably white-tailed deer, have rebounded in the area.

The Interior Lowlands Belt of South Texas, stretching from Austin to San Antonio to Uvalde, contains soil that is highly prized for farming. However, in some areas, very little natural vegetation remains as a result of this farming and of real estate development. For this reason, the National Wildlife Refuge System, the Audubon Society, and the Nature Conservancy have established several wildlife refuges in the area, which help protect endangered animals and plants native to the United States that have lost their habitats to agriculture. Endangered animals in the area include the ocelot, the jaguarundi, and the mountain lion, though mountain lions are not officially protected. Even without protection, sightings indicate that mountain lions inhabit more counties now than they did ten years ago, and they appear to be expanding their range into Central Texas.

The Lower Rio Grande Valley National Wildlife Refuge was established in 1980 and is still a work in progress. It stretches across four counties—Starr, Hidalgo, Cameron, and Willacy—and will encompass 107,500 acres when completed. Brasil, Texas ebony, and anacua trees thrive here. The Sabal Palm Forest contains jungle-like stands of *Sabal texana*, the palm for which the Rio de las Palmas (Rio Grande) was named in 1519. Many animals have already found sanctuary in this refuge, which also provides critical habitat for more than 400 species of migrating birds. Environmentalists hope that the completion of this refuge will prevent the extinction of many animals and plants that might otherwise be lost forever.

Another refuge, the Rio Grande–Falcon Thorn Woodland, stretches about 20 miles southeast from Falcon Dam along the lower Rio Grande River. Consisting of 24,000 acres, this stretch of the river harbors rare tropical-thorn woodland and is recognized nationally as an important sanctuary for fish and wildlife. Many migrating and native birds inhabit the area, including the hook-billed kite. The only native stand of Montezuma bald cypress trees in Texas can be found here as well.

A little farther down the Rio Grande, Chihuahua Woods Preserve is a refuge that remains largely in its native state, despite the development that has taken place around it. More than 90 percent of the Rio Grande floodplain has been converted to cropland, and, as reported at the Nature Conservancy's website (www.nature.org), "less than 5 percent of [the] original habitat remains in its native condition." Chihuahua Woods is thus unique. The preserve, which is managed by the Nature Conservancy, showcases a wide variety of native plant species, including a particularly impressive community of cacti.

I visited Chihuahua Woods on a steamy March day a few years ago, while researching a story for *Texas Highways* magazine. The sign posted at the entrance to the refuge was enough to give me second thoughts about entering: THORNS, CACTI, INSECTS AND POISONOUS SNAKES ARE COMMON HERE. SOME HAZARDS MAY BE UNFAMILIAR TO YOU. BE AWARE THAT AFRICANIZED (i.e., killer) BEES MAY BE PRESENT. RABIES IS PREVALENT IN SOUTH TEXAS. DO NOT HANDLE ANY DEAD ANIMAL. And worst of all: NO RESTROOM FACILITIES ARE AVAILABLE.

Retama tree in full bloom,
Webb County

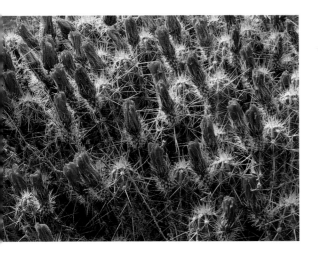

Having grown up in and survived South Texas, I decided to ignore common sense and press ahead anyway. My fervent desire was not only to catch a glimpse of the elusive jaguarundis and/or ocelots said to frequent the area, but also to see the exotic cacti I had heard so much about. I checked my water supply, packed a couple of extra towels, and slung on my backpack. I proceeded through the gate, flinging caution to the wind. Not so bad, I thought, after walking for ten minutes without sustaining any more damage than a shirt saturated with perspiration.

Knee-high grass gave way to mesquite thickets and cenizo—typical thornscrub vegetation. Then came prickly pear (opuntia) in droves: undulate, nopal, Indian fig, and cochineal. Trying to avoid the treacherous prickly pear, I grazed another spiny terror, the tasajillo, or Christmas cactus, that is always waiting to grab the careless, unfortunate hiker. The tasajillo cactus has a much different appearance than the prickly pear cactus, though they are members of the same family. Instead of thick, wide pads, the tasajillo has long, thin branches studded with sharp, hooked spines, which allows it to hide under the cover of another plant. The unwary hiker seldom sees it coming, unless it is growing out in the open. Brush up against the plant even slightly and the barbs grab hold of clothing and skin. The opportunistic plant then releases a segment of itself, hitching a free ride on an unfortunate victim and thereby increasing its chances for reproduction.

After five minutes of daintily pulling spiky segments of the offending plant off of my pants, shirt, and boots, I continued on—wiser, more careful, and resolute not to suffer another close encounter with the treacherous tasajillo. As I forged ahead, I noticed more cactus species: dog cholla, pencil cactus, horse crippler, pincushions, fishhook barrel, and the sprawling strawberry pitaya cactus.

The strawberry cactus is one I find particularly intriguing. A large number of these specimens were growing in a small field and looked very robust due to recent rains. The arms of the cactus reach out in all directions from the central root area, much like the serpents that grew from the mythological Medusa's head. The cacti were bright green with yellowish spines, and each branch was studded with a shriveled, wine-colored blossom. It appeared as if I had missed the bloom by just a few days, but the color contrasts were still beautiful, and I made a few exposures before moving on.

South Texas breeds hardy souls. Early explorers found out soon after arriving here that it takes a special kind of mettle to compete with the tough, specially adapted plants and animals that have survived here for thousands of years. The Brush Country of today is a mere shadow of its former self, a patchwork of thorny woodlands and cattle pastures interspersed with small towns and crisscrossed with asphalt highways and caliche back roads. The thornscrub has been tamed for the most part by ranchers, but you know it's just waiting to take over again if we stall in our efforts to subdue it. I, for one, would like to see that happen.

Above
Huisache daisies, verbena, and fleabane cover tire tracks in Medina County

Facing page
Bluebonnets, phlox, and dandelions flower near a live oak tree, Atascosa County

Above
Spanish moss drapes trees along a
Resaca, Santa Ana National
Wildlife Refuge

Left
Turk's cap grows beneath palm trees at
Sabal Palm Audubon Sanctuary

Far left
Sunset at Santa Ana National
Wildlife Refuge

Above
A sprawling prickly pear thicket thrives
in Chihuahua Woods Preserve

Right
An armadillo stops to pick up a scent,
San Patricio County

A strawberry cactus with spent blossoms, Chihuahua Woods Preserve

Chapter 6

THE TRANS-PECOS

SPRAWLING DESERTS, JAGGED MOUNTAINS, AND ENDLESS VISTAS

Above
Remains of an agave in the Chisos Mountains,
Big Bend National Park

Left
Agaves and a juniper skeleton on the South Rim,
Big Bend National Park

Rainbow cactus, Brewster County

W EST TEXAS, THE Trans-Pecos, Big Bend Country, and God's Country are some of the names given to this part of Texas that lies within the Basin and Range province, one of the major physiographic regions of North America. The land here has not radically changed from how it was hundreds of years ago, when Apaches and Mexicans were among the few who dared attempt to scratch out an existence here. Though ribbons of asphalt now stretch across the harsh desert and wind through forbidding mountains, and overgrazing has transformed grasslands into deserts, Big Bend Country is still relatively unspoiled compared to most other regions in Texas. Windmills, ramshackle barns, and occasional small towns dot this vast area, but for the most part, the landscape remains intact.

The Trans-Pecos lies west of the Pecos River within the Chihuahuan Desert, one of four major deserts in the United States. Most of the desert rests in Mexico, but it extends into southern New Mexico, southeastern Arizona, and southwestern Texas. The Chihuahuan Desert is a land of high elevations, ranging from 1,000 feet near the Rio Grande to 5,500 feet along the foothills of the mountain ranges.

Many of the thirty mountain ranges in West Texas are fault-block mountains, created when large masses of the earth's crust were forced upward over time and tilted to the side. In between fault-block ranges are large basins called bolsons, where rivers pool into lakes. Originally, the mountain peaks were much taller than they are now and the basins were much deeper, but nature has a way of leveling things out over time. Millions of years of rain, wind, freezing temperatures, and gravity have softened the jagged peaks and transferred the eroded minerals, gravel, and dirt to the basins. At first, these sprawling, ephemeral lakebeds were closed off, surrounded on all sides by the mountains, but over time the two largest rivers in West Texas, the Pecos and Rio Grande, cut through the basins, providing drainage. The rivers carried sand, gravel, and salts downstream, eventually depositing them into the sea.

Extensive populations of creosote bush and tarbush are found in the Chihuahuan Desert, along with mesquite trees, yuccas, agaves, and a menagerie of cacti. The lechuguilla, a type of agave, is unique to this desert; it is not indigenous to any other region on Earth. Agaves are a low-growing plant with thick, rigid leaves that terminate in a sharp point. They can take up to forty years to mature and, upon maturation, they expend all their energy producing a spectacular flower, and then they die. Agaves have been used through the years as food, to make rope, and to make soap.

Cacti are perhaps the best-known desert plants. In the Trans-Pecos, they are found in all shapes and sizes, ranging from the deftly camouflaged living rock cactus, which grows barely above ground level, to the rangy prickly pears, which can grow as tall as 8 feet and, where conditions are favorable, form nearly impenetrable stands. The spines of a cactus help the plant conserve water in the arid desert environment, while the fruit of many cacti serve as a valuable food source for animals (and people too) and the sticky flesh of the pads has been used by Native Americans to bind wounds or as an anesthetic. Cacti blooms are spectacular and appear in a

A cane cholla cactus in full bloom, Big Bend National Park

variety of colors, depending on the species. The most prolific blooms occur between March and May, but there are some species that flower during summer, fall, or late-winter.

Opuntias are by far the most abundant cacti in the Trans-Pecos, with sixteen species falling within two varieties: chollas or prickly pears. Opuntias begin to bloom in March and can continue to bloom into June. The purple-tinged prickly pear forms a striking presence in the otherwise drab desert environment, putting forth spectacular yellow flowers with blood-red centers. The brilliant blossoms of the chollas, which range from deep purples to yellows and white, generally begin to open in late April. Though not as abundant as prickly pears, their bright color makes them stand out on the desert floor.

Human history in the Trans-Pecos is scattered and sparse, the harshness of the environment and the scarcity of resources there having little to offer human settlers. Some of the earliest inhabitants lived in the area more than 10,000 years ago, but these Paleo-Indians left behind little evidence of their existence, so not much is known about them. Scientists know more about two other cultures, the Archaic and

Neo-American peoples. The Archaic culture flourished between approximately 7000 B.C. and 500 A.D., while the Neo-American peoples inhabited the area between about 500 A.D. and the arrival of the Spanish in the early 1500s. Both groups were nomadic hunter-gatherers who roamed the area in search of plant- and animal-based food. By the time of the Neo-Americans, however, there was a greater dependence on agriculture, and toward the end of this culture, more-permanent human settlements had come into existence.

Spanish influence in the Big Bend area began around 1535, when Spanish colonists and explorers moved north from Mexico into what would later become Texas. The Spaniards first tried enslaving the indigenous peoples, and then established the mission system to "civilize" and Christianize the desert tribes, including the Tobosas, Salineros, Tepehuanes, and Cabezas. When the Apaches arrived in the area during the 1600s and then the Comanches in the early 1700s, the Spaniards found themselves on the defensive as these tribes revolted. Comanche raids became so frequent that officials from New Spain almost conceded the northern country to the Native Americans.

By 1790, however, the majority of Apaches had withdrawn from Texas, with only a few small bands remaining in strongholds in the Chisos and Davis mountains. The Comanches, meanwhile, focused their efforts on Big Bend country. By the time the United States won possession of the Big Bend region from Mexico in 1848, the U.S. army had constructed a line of forts along travel routes through Texas that eventually resulted in controlling the activities of the remaining Native Americans.

Purple-tinged prickly pear, Big Bend National Park

A long-spined prickly pear flowers amid sotols and agaves in Pine Canyon, Big Bend National Park

Around 1885, serious overgrazing of the Big Bend grasslands began with the arrival of the Estacado Land and Cattle Company. As many as 30,000 head of cattle roamed Big Bend country at one time, and with Estacado's success, dozens of smaller operators moved into the area in subsequent years to take advantage of grazing opportunities. By the late 1920s, the once-lush grasslands had been depleted all the way up to the Chisos highlands.

At around the same time, mining operations were established in the Terlingua and Mariscal areas to extract quicksilver. It wasn't until 1935 that the U.S. Congress passed legislation enabling the acquisition of 708,221 acres in the Big Bend region, with the intent of restoring the land to the condition it was in before Europeans arrived. On June 12, 1944, all ranching, agriculture, and mining operations within this acreage ceased, and Big Bend National Park was born.

Visitors might be tempted to think that Big Bend's isolation and remoteness would spare it from environmental problems plaguing other wild places, such as Grand Canyon or Yosemite national parks. Unfortunately, in the past few decades, air pollution has become a major concern in West Texas. Dirty air drifts in from a number of sources, including Monterrey and Monclova in northern Mexico;

Mexico City; and Houston and Galveston, Texas. Windblown soil and dust also contribute to poor visibility.

Though on a good day a hiker can still stand at the precipice of the South Rim, which affords the grandest view in all of Big Bend, and see mountains in Mexico more than 100 miles away, the poor air quality in the park frequently limits that view to 30 miles or less. Landscape photographers notice the visual effects of air pollution when they get their film back from the lab and see a dirty brown band hugging the horizon in their pictures. The film tends to exaggerate the effect, but make no mistake, the stuff exists. Photographers are also quick to notice that the very earliest light of sunrise or the last light of sunset, known as "sweet light," is not as clear and sharp as it used to be.

Efforts are underway to clean the air in Big Bend, and in the other national parks and wilderness areas in the state of Texas and beyond. In 1999, a Regional Haze Rule was enacted by the Environmental Protection Agency, which, according to the National Park Service website (www. nps.gov), "calls for state and federal agencies to work together to improve visibility . . . [to] reach natural background conditions within the next sixty years." Also in 1999, the Environmental Protection Agency and the National Park Service combined forces to conduct an extensive air pollution study called the Big Bend Regional Aerosol and Visibility Observational study (BRAVO). The ultimate goal of the study is to determine the source(s) and components of air pollution in the park, which will hopefully lead to solutions that can be implemented to improve the air quality and visibility within the park.

Above
Claret cup cactus blossoms, Brewster County

Facing page
A claret cup cactus blooms on the South Rim, Big Bend National Park

The Davis Mountains region, in the heart of West Texas, could be described as a kinder, gentler version of Big Bend. The mountains are older and more worn and the plant life is less thorny than in Big Bend, and the relatively mild climate is one of the best in Texas. Ponderosa pine, quaking aspens, pinyon pine, gray oak, alligator juniper, and mountain mahogany are all found in this region, as are eleven rare species of plants. The Davis Mountains, in fact, are home to one of the most biologically diverse ecosystems in Texas. As in so many other areas in the state, however, this region has suffered land abuses such as overgrazing and habitat fragmentation, and an increasing human population has put a strain on limited water resources. The Nature Conservancy has stepped forward to help curb these trends, by purchasing 18,277 acres in the heart of the mountains and by securing conservation easements on 65,830 acres of adjoining property. Their hope is to preserve the biodiversity of the area, to prevent habitat fragmentation, and to stop light pollution from impeding important research taking place at the University of Texas McDonald Observatory, situated atop the mountains.

The Guadalupe Mountains, which rise from the desert 110 miles east of El Paso, harbor parts of a prehistoric fossil reef that contains remnants of marine organisms such as algae, sponges, brachiopods, crinoids, and coral that lived and died

Above
Desert sunrise from South Rim, Big Bend National Park

Facing page, top left
Rime cloaks a juniper tree and agave in ice, Big Bend National Park

Facing page, top right
Frosty foliage in the Chisos Basin, Big Bend National Park

Facing page, bottom
A cenizo blooms after summer rains, Big Bend National Park

in the sea that once covered most of Texas. This mountain range also features the highest mountain peak in Texas (the 8,749-foot Guadalupe Peak), and its rugged, arid quality belies the beauty and diversity that lies within. McKittrick Canyon shelters forests of pine and relict populations of bigtooth maple trees watered by pristine mountain streams. Mini-sanctuaries and grottos within the mountains support a variety of plant and animal life, including mountain lions, mule deer, kit foxes, maidenhair fern, and a host of flora and fauna that have learned how to survive and flourish in the extreme climate and topography of West Texas.

Overall, the Trans-Pecos region is rich in biodiversity, showcases some awe-inspiring scenery, and is home to unique plant and animal life found nowhere else in Texas. It is perhaps surprising that the rural counties are still sparsely populated, though the El Paso region in particular continues its steady growth. We can only hope, however, that efforts by the park systems, by wildlife organizations, and by concerned individuals will enable this region to retain its relatively unspoiled qualities as we tackle difficult issues like air pollution, overgrazing, and habitat fragmentation.

Below
Big Bend bluebonnets and prickly pear adorn a ravine, Big Bend National Park

Right
Lush stipa grass carpets a meadow in Green Gulch, Big Bend National Park

A thunderstorm approaches the badlands of Big Bend National Park

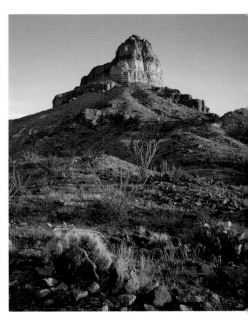

Above, top
Sunset-tinged storm clouds
color the skies above Big
Bend National Park

Above, bottom
Ocotillo, prickly pear, and
strawberry cacti at the base
of Cerro Castolon, Big
Bend National Park

Right
Cemetery at Terlingua ghost town,
Brewster County

Below
View from Mount Locke,
Davis Mountains

Facing page
Scarlet bouvardia blooms after summer
rains, Davis Mountains

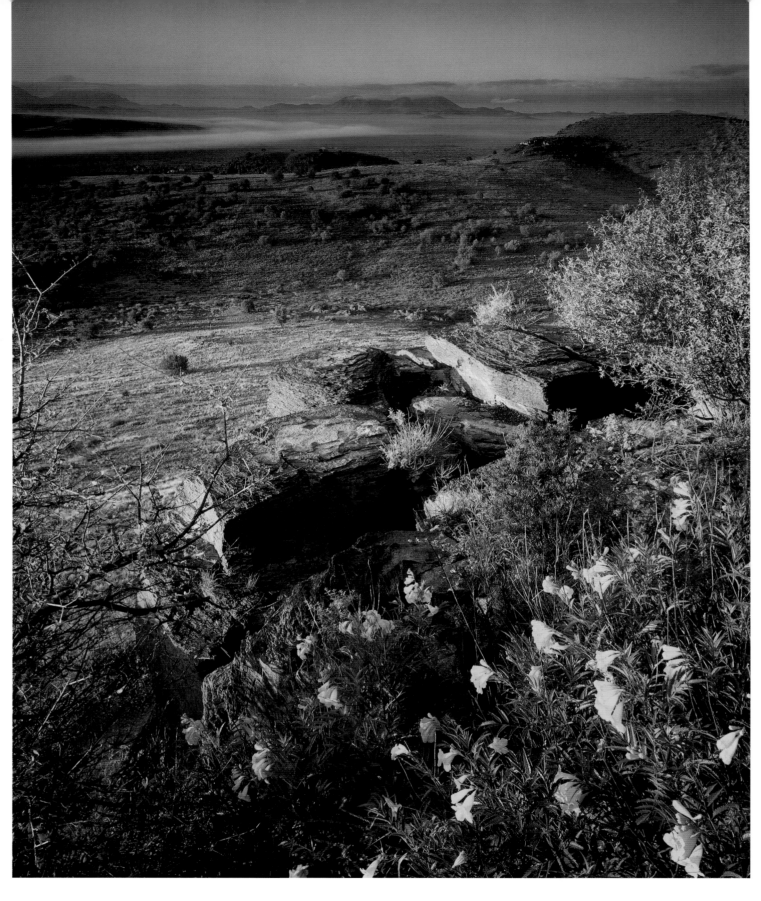

A Davis Mountains vista with Esperanza and scarlet bouvardia in bloom, Fort Davis National Historic Site

Far left
Cottonwood trees with a dusting of snow, Davis Mountains

Left
A pair of cottonwood trees glow in afternoon light, Jeff Davis County

Sawtooth Mountain and frost-tinged trees, Jeff Davis County

Above
Stipa grass and maple tree in Dog
Canyon, Guadalupe Mountains
National Park

Right
Maple leaves adorn limestone boulders
in Dog Canyon, Guadalupe Mountains
National Park

Facing page
A palette of autumn colors bright-
ens McKittrick Canyon, Guadalupe
Mountains National Park

Maple leaves and ferns at Smith Spring, Guadalupe Mountains National Park

Left
Pictographs, Seminole Canyon
State Park

Below
Patterns in the sand, Monahans
Sandhills State Park

Chapter 7

OAK WOODS AND PRAIRIES

THE BUFFALO'S DOMAIN

Above
Rose gentians and a solitary
Indian paintbrush bloom, Austin County

Left
Coreopsis surrounds a trio of old wagons,
Gonzales County

ONE DAY LATE in May, I decide to take a photo trip into the Blackland Prairie region of Texas. I don't have to go very far, since the prairie begins just a few miles east of where I live in Austin. This particular day, I am interested in a specific parcel of authentic prairie known as Clymer Meadow Preserve, which has somehow managed to avoid development for decades—unlike the vast majority of the prairie lands around it.

I arrive at the preserve before sunrise to take advantage of the warm, glowing first-light of day. The weather is uncharacteristically cool, due to an abnormally wet and mild spring. There is a slight breeze, which is never helpful when you're photographing flowers, grass, or anything else that can blow in the wind. In this part of the state, however, wind is to be expected almost anytime, so I've learned to work with it. I determine that I'm not going to have crystal-clear light this day; there is a thin layer of cirrus clouds in the eastern sky that diffuses the golden sunlight like a large studio scrim. In the end, however, the conditions are ideal for what I'm photographing this morning.

The meadow before me is different from anything I have photographed before. Tall, deep-green grasses sway lazily in the cool morning breeze, contrasting beautifully with a few purple Indian paintbrushes scattered throughout the field. With no sound other than the long-stemmed grasses rustling in the breeze and a cow bellowing in the distance, the setting is very pastoral. As the morning sunlight intensifies—skimming the tops of the tallest grasses, and bathing the entire meadow in a warm glow—I make a number of exposures.

Clymer Meadow Preserve encompasses about 1,000 acres in far north-central Texas, near the Oklahoma border. The site was named for Jim Clymer, a pioneer who purchased the first tracts of land here in the mid 1800s. The preserve harbors one of the few remaining remnants of Blackland Prairie, a tallgrass prairie that once flourished from southern Canada all the way to the Gulf of Mexico. Of the 12 million acres of original Blackland Prairie that once existed within the state of Texas alone, only 5,000 acres remain, scattered on small parcels throughout the state.

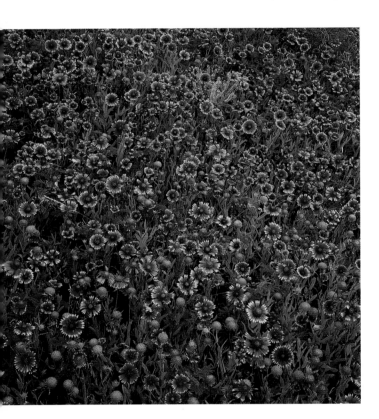

Gaillardia blankets a clearing,
Hagerman National Wildlife Refuge

Much of this prairie land is voluntarily protected under a private land registry program administered by the Nature Conservancy. Clymer Meadow Preserve represents one of the best intact parcels still in existence in Texas.

Before European settlement in the early to mid 1800s, the prairie was a disturbance-maintained ecosystem, with climate, naturally occurring fires, and periodic grazing by bison, antelope, and other large herbivores helping to maintain the grasslands. In the early 1800s, however, settlers began to plow and cultivate the land. The rich, fertile soil of the prairie was ideal for agriculture, the lifeblood of many early Texas settlements.

The vast majority of the original Texas Blackland Prairie today is in fact dominated by farming and ranching interests, while other parts of the prairie have seen

Morning light at Clymer Meadow, Hunt County

urban development. The cities of San Antonio, Austin, Temple, Waco, and Dallas were all built on prairie grasslands. The specter of additional development makes this region one of North America's most imperiled ecosystems.

Clymer Meadow Preserve not only protects a parcel of the original Blackland Prairie, it also functions as an educational site, where scientists and researchers can study the plants that best suit the prairie land, the conditions under which the prairie will thrive, and the relationships between the prairie plants and the native wildlife. These studies assist scientists in their attempts to save other remnants of original prairie and also help them to foster environments where new prairies can grow. For example, in 1999 a small herd of bison was reintroduced to Clymer Meadow on an experimental basis, marking the first time in 150 years that bison have roamed these lands. This experiment allows researchers to study the effects of the grazing bison on the prairie and determine whether such an arrangement makes for a healthier prairie.

Clymer Meadow Preserve also serves as a teaching site where students and the public at large can learn about the native plants and about the importance of preserving them. The site is home to more than 250 kinds of plants, including thriving communities of little bluestem-Indiangrass and gamagrass-switchgrass. Big bluestem, meadow dropseed, sideoats grama, and Canada wild rye also flourish here, as well as a number of wildflowers, including purple coneflower, rough-leaf rosinweed, prairie clover, and American basketflower.

Other Blackland Prairie sites with impressive wildflower displays include Fort Parker State Park, near the town of Mexia, which has planted a native prairie demonstration site sown with native grasses and wildflowers that grow in the soils of the region, such as bluebonnet, purple vetch, partridge pea, prairie larkspur, and baby blue eyes. Lake Mineral Wells State Park and Trailway features blooms typical of the Western Cross Timbers vegetational zone. Some of the best places to view the wildflowers in this park are along the roadway, from the Cross Timbers hike and bike trail, and along the state trailway, which runs for 20 miles between Mineral Wells and Weatherford.

The Eastern and Western Cross Timbers stretch along either side of the Blackland Prairie region. These narrow bands of forest run parallel to one another for about 160 miles from the Oklahoma border south into Central Texas, harboring stands of post oak and blackjack oak, among other vegetation. The forests of the Cross Timbers served as both a barrier and a landmark for early travelers, who gave the region its name due to their repeated "crossings" through the densely "timbered" land. Many Native American tribes harvested the plentiful wood of the region and used the area as a north-south thoroughfare that offered protection from their enemies.

Today, the forests of the Eastern Cross Timbers are denser and the trees generally taller than those in the Western Cross Timbers because the soil in the eastern region is more fertile, with the western region showcasing more exposed rock. The

Winecups and Engelmann's daisies,
Milam County

vegetation in the eastern region is more diverse for the same reason. Both forests help conserve water in the area by preventing water from running-off too rapidly after it rains. The trees from both forests continue to be harvested.

Dinosaur Valley State Park is a 1,524-acre preserve within the Western Cross Timbers region. The Paluxy riverbed that runs through the park is home to some world-famous fossilized dinosaur tracks, which are best viewed in late summer, when water levels in the river are usually lowest. Scientists believe the tracks were made by two-legged, carnivorous theropods and four-legged, herbivorous sauropods. The larger footprints are believed to have been made by a pleurocoelus, a type of sauropod that grew up to 50 feet long.

In the far southwestern reaches of the Blackland Prairie region, Palmetto State Park harbors a botanical area unique to the state. Dense stands of dwarf palmetto palms, which give the park its name, generate a tropical feel, belying the park's proximity to the prairie. The diverse flora and fauna here are representative of the lands directly east and west of the park. In springtime, red buckeye, purple iris, spiderwort, and crimson Drummond phlox transform the monochromatic green woodlands into a blaze of color.

The rolling oak woodlands of the Post Oak Belt and parts of the Blackland Prairie separate the anomalous but beautiful "Lost Pines of Texas" from the main pine forest in East Texas. These isolated loblolly pines are preserved in Bastrop State Park and are part of the most westerly stand of loblolly pines in the state. The ancestors of these trees are believed to have been part of a vast prehistoric pine forest. As land areas gradually rose, possibly due to glacial activity during the last ice age, the main body of the pine forest moved east, leaving behind this isolated pocket of trees. Plentiful rains and mild winters have kept the grove intact over time.

Despite all that the oak woods and prairies region has to offer, one of its most endearing views has to be the stunning wildflower displays that occur here, particularly during wet years. An elegant prairie wildflower that I find particularly beautiful is the Texas bluebell, sometimes called *Lira de San Pedro*, which grows sporadically in sunny, moist places across most of the state, but which reserves its most spectacular displays for the prairies of southeastern Texas. The flowers are large and showy, sometimes reaching 4 inches across and 2 feet in height, and are usually bluish purple with yellow pistils and stamens.

As I take leave of this region, I recall an early July day several years ago, when I received a call from a woman who lives in Fayette County, on the southeastern edge of the Blackland Prairie. She called to tell me that her pasture was full of bluebells and she thought the occasion merited having a professional photograph made. Up to that time, I had only photographed a few bluebells scattered here and there throughout the Hill Country, so the opportunity to capture a field of them on film was impossible to resist. With directions to her property in hand, I left my house the next day two hours before dawn so that I could take advantage of the early morning light.

As I veered from the main highway and traveled down a gravel road for about a mile, I wondered if I would be able to find her property. But when I reached the crest of a small hill, the spectacle that unfolded before me left no doubt that I had indeed found the place. A landscape stretched out before me of gently rolling green pastures covered with thousands of tall bluebells swaying lazily in a light breeze. After walking through the elegant flowers in a somewhat stunned state for fifteen minutes or so, I realized that, before the sun rose, I needed to select a vantage point from which to take my picture. With dozens of possibilities racing through my mind, I finally decided on an angle that would include a tin shed in the background, and I set up my 4x5-inch view camera. After just a few minutes, the sun cleared a hill behind me, the wind miraculously relented for a few minutes, and I was able to make my exposures. I have been back to that spot almost every year since I took that picture and there has never been another bloom that even remotely matched the extravagant show nature put on that year.

View from a scenic overlook in the Post Oak Belt, Gonzales County

Coreopsis flowers along the Paluxy River, Dinosaur Valley State Park

Left
Sunlight highlights a dwarf palmetto, Palmetto State Park

Below, left
Red buckeye blooms amid dwarf palmettos at Palmetto State Park

Below
Red buckeye flowers, Palmetto State Park

Right and below
Ferns grace the forest floor at Bastrop
State Park, Bastrop County

Facing page
Loblolly pine saplings, Bastrop State
Park, Bastrop County

Far left
Field of bluebell gentians,
Fayette County

Left, top
Drummond phlox, bluebonnets, chick-
weed and primrose create a tapestry of
primary colors, Gonzales County

Left, bottom
Indian paintbrush and bluebonnets
bloom in a church yard in
Bastrop County

Chapter 8

PRESERVING OUR HERITAGE FOR THE FUTURE

Above
Winecups and gaillardia, Blanco County

Left
A field of bluebonnets, Indian paintbrush, and
Ashe junipers near Lake Buchanan,
Llano County

I HAVE BEEN photographing the Texas landscape since I was eighteen years old. Back then, I had not traveled beyond the state's borders, so my idea of how the rest of the world looked was based on photographs I saw in books and magazines. I was first influenced by the work of Josef Muench, who made so many memorable photographs of Arizona's natural wonders for *Arizona Highways* magazine. His images, which depicted vast landscapes of great strength and beauty, inspired me to develop a strong connection to the land.

I soon discovered the work of Ansel Adams and Eliot Porter. Their work displayed perfection of the highest order, in nature, in artistic vision, and in technical prowess. Adams worked primarily in black and white, while Porter's images were in color. As I traveled both within Texas and outside the state, I photographed some of the same subjects that my predecessors had captured on film so many years ago. In the process, I discovered that many of the views depicted in their work had changed, some just a little, and others drastically. In some places, natural processes such as fire, drought, and the natural cycles of life were responsible for the changes. In most cases, however, human intervention had brought about the changes—urban and agricultural development had replaced woodlands and grasslands, and rivers had been dammed to create reservoirs.

I began to realize that the land has changed dramatically over the span of just one generation, and I've begun to wonder what will be left for the next generation to enjoy, marvel at, and photograph. In Texas, millions of acres of grasslands have been converted for agricultural use or for urbanization. Large cities now cover more than 4 million acres in Texas—twice as much area as what is occupied by public lands, parks, refuges, and preserves. Natural landscapes have been altered and exotic species have been introduced, creating an imbalance in the local biotic community.

Much of the wildlife native to Texas—deer, mountain lions, antelope, bighorn sheep—requires large habitat areas in which to live and thrive, and ironically, the large ranches of past generations provided such habitat. Cattle roamed in relatively undisturbed lands eating what nature provided. Because most ranches were managed in the same low-impact manner, large tracts of native habitat were preserved. Our farming and ranching history is part of the heritage that makes Texas what it is today. It is a tradition that has played a large part in preserving the land, and it must continue for Texas to retain its identity.

Fragmentation occurs when these large farms and ranches are divided into smaller parcels, disrupting the environment. With more farmers and ranchers on the land, water demands increase, open space is diminished, wildlife habitat is destroyed, and water quality is compromised due to erosion and run-off. Each year since 1970, about 1,000 new farms and ranches have been established in Texas. Between 1992 and 2002 alone, more than half a million acres of

Horse drive below El Capitan, Guadalupe Mountains National Park

Volcanic rubble contrasts with white tuff at Cerro Castolon, Big Bend National Park

farm and ranchland were converted to land uses other than agriculture (recreation, real estate development, urbanization).

Part of the problem with land fragmentation is that parcels of land are sold to people who have grown up in or near cities, people who have generally not developed the close ties to the land that previous generations had. City life provides a kind of insular protection from, and lack of understanding of, the ecological importance of wild lands. Many landowners arrive with good intentions, but not enough basic knowledge of wildlife and land management techniques to be good land stewards. The resulting land management practices often have devastating results on the flora and fauna of the area.

Why should we care about preserving Texas's wild lands? On the most elementary level, the loss of biodiversity—the variety of all life forms and their ecosystems—is not reversible. Humans have the ability to halt the deterioration of the physical environment (though it would be a monumental task), but the loss of unique organisms and species is out of our control. Earth has undergone five great extinctions over the past 500 million years. The sixth is occurring right now at the hands of humans. Harvard professor and sociobiologist Edward O. Wilson believes that one-fifth of all species of plant and animal organisms (numbering between 10 million and 100 million) could be forever lost by the year 2020. According to Wilson we should consider every species of plant and animal priceless until we can ascertain its value to the entire ecosystem.

We must have reliable, dependable sources of water. Over the years, the issue of water and water rights has proven to be a lightning rod of controversy in Texas. Groundwater and the water that fills our lakes and streams are not infinite resources, and we must make every effort to protect and preserve them. Proper stewardship of our water resources is also necessary to control erosion and flooding.

Preservation of ecological communities is also essential. We depend on plants and animals for our survival. We are not separate from the forests, deserts, wetlands, and prairies of our state; we are part of them. If we allow degradation of natural habitats that sustain wildlife, we are robbing our descendants of resources that they should rightly expect and enjoy.

Nature preserves, parks, and other scenic areas raise nearby land values and are important factors in contributing to the quality of life of all people. On the economic side, they are also necessary for recreation and tourism, which is one of the largest sources of revenue in Texas.

There are a number of programs that could be implemented, or are already being implemented, to rescue Texas's wild lands. Land trusts, for example, are local, state, or regional nonprofit organizations that conserve land for its recreational, scenic, and historical values, as well as for the protection of wildlife. The trusts secure key land parcels donated or sold by willing landowners and ensure that these lands will be preserved for generations to come. The government sometimes even provides incentives in the form of tax breaks to landowners who donate land. Land trusts can provide local solutions to local needs, such as protection of a watershed, a prairie, or an archaeological resource. Some important land trusts in Texas are Audubon Texas, Bat Conservation International, and the Galveston Bay Foundation.

Purchase of Development Rights (PDR) programs also are helping preserve the wild lands of Texas, by curtailing land fragmentation and preventing damage to native habitats, ranches, and farms. PDR programs purchase development rights from willing landowners in order to preserve natural resources and maintain wildlife habitat areas while concurrently preserving our farming and ranching heritage. PDR programs greatly reduce the costs of land and water conservation, since the cost of a PDR is much less than the cost of purchasing the land for conventional use. As of this writing, a PDR program was proposed in the Texas legislature but did not pass.

Sunrise at Santa Ana National
Wildlife Refuge

The Nature Conservancy has been saving wild lands, plants, and animals in Texas since 1964. They have acquired and oversee thirty-four Texas nature preserves and manage an additional sixty-one conservation projects in the state, all the while protecting from development more than 900,000 acres of important habitat.

For example, deep in the Rio Grande Valley, the Conservancy has acquired Southmost Preserve, which harbors one of the last stands of native sabal palm trees in the country. In a region that has historically been used primarily for agricultural purposes, the Conservancy has provided sanctuary for this unique area that is sometimes called the "Jewel of the Rio Grande Valley."

In the late 1980s, the Lennox family donated to the Conservancy the breathtaking area now known as Lennox Woods Preserve, a mixed evergreen-deciduous forest in far northeastern Texas that provides habitat for many important plant and animal communities. These woodlands are believed to be classic examples of what existed in the area prior to the arrival of European settlers.

Water rushes over limestone boulders at Twin Falls on Barton Creek, Travis County

Another Conservancy acquisition, the Roy E. Larsen Sandyland Sanctuary is a 5,500-acre preserve in the heart of the Big Thicket region in eastern Texas. Honoring Roy E. Larsen, a lifelong conservationist, the sanctuary contains an amazing array of flora and fauna that thrive in the swamplands and southern pine forests found here. The Nature Conservancy acquired this property as part of its goal to preserve and restore longleaf pine forests, one of "the most rapidly disappearing ecosystems in the southeastern United States," according to the Conservancy's website (www.nature. org). Due to heavy logging, farming, and real estate development, only a mere 3 percent of the original 70 million acres of this once robust ecosystem remains.

Environmental Defense is another nonprofit organization committed to helping solve critical environmental problems in Texas and throughout the nation. In Texas they have launched a program to aid private landowners interested in restoring and managing habitat for two endangered songbirds—the black-capped vireo and the golden-cheeked warbler—that nest on ranches in the Texas Hill Country. This initiative, called the Landowner Conservation Assistance Program, is appropriate for owners who wish to enhance habitat and protect wildlife without placing long-term restrictions on their property. Environmental Defense has recently expanded the program to include the endangered ocelot, whose primary habitat is in South Texas.

Yet another nonprofit organization, the Conservation Fund, has protected more than 90,000 acres in Texas, including 20,000 acres in the Rio Grande Valley; 3,900 acres of critical dunes and wetlands along the coast; and 50,000 acres in the Fort Davis area of West Texas. The Fund is currently working toward protecting 33,000 acres of bottomland hardwood and longleaf forest along the Neches River.

The 1996 Farm Bill enacted by the U.S. Congress established a new program called the Wildlife Habitat Incentive Program. From 1996 through 2002, 50 million dollars has been appropriated to assist landowners around the country with wildlife protection and conservation activities. The U.S. Department of Agriculture (USDA) Natural Resources Conservation Service in Temple administers the program in Texas. The program targets wildlife-habitat restoration activities, including restoration of prairies, savannas, wetlands, and other riparian habitats. As of 2002, Texas landowners had more than 30,000 acres of habitat in the program.

The Farm Bill's Conservation Reserve Program is a voluntary cost-share program that allows landowners to enter into ten- or fifteen-year contracts with the USDA to take environmentally sensitive lands out of production in an effort to preserve wildlife habitat. In 2002, more than 4 million acres in Texas were protected under the program.

The Texas Wetlands Conservation Plan, initiated by Texas Parks and Wildlife in 1994, seeks to preserve and protect some of Texas's most endangered and valuable areas. Wetlands provide many economic and ecological benefits, including flood control, improved water quality, harvestable products, and habitat for fish and

shellfish. The program utilizes voluntary, nonregulatory approaches to conserving Texas's remaining wetlands. The plan works by enhancing landowners' abilities to use existing incentive programs; developing and encouraging land management options that provide economic incentives for conserving and restoring wetlands; and coordinating regional wetland conservation efforts.

Although much has been done to preserve and protect Texas land and resources, there are still too many areas at risk of being lost to development, degradation, or neglect. A number of organizations and dedicated people are working to save our special places, but it will require the will and resolve of the majority of Texans, not just a small group of them, to ensure that our descendants will be able to enjoy and benefit from Texas's wild lands.

Dogwood, sassafras, and grape leaves brighten the forest floor, Caddo Lake State Park

Yuccas silhouetted against a fiery sky, Laguna Atascosa National Wildlife Refuge

CONSERVATION ORGANIZATIONS

American Farmland Trust
1200 18th Street NW
Washington, D.C. 20036
202.331.7300
http://www.farmland.org/texas
index.htm

Audubon Texas
901 South Mopac
Building II, Ste. 410
Austin, TX 78746
512.306.0225
http://www.tx.audubon.org/about/
contact.htm

Bayou Preservation Association
P.O. Box 131563
Houston, TX 77219-1563
713.529.6443
http://www.bayoupreservation.org/

Big Thicket Association
P.O. Box 198
Saratoga, Texas 77585
http://www.btatx.org/

Environmental Defense, Texas
44 East Avenue, Suite 304
Austin, TX 78701
512.478.5161
http://www.environmentaldefense
.org/home.cfm

Katy Prairie Conservancy
3015 Richmond Avenue, Suite 230
Houston, TX 77098
713.523.6135
http://www.katyprairie.org/

Land Trust Alliance
Southwest Region
115 North Fifth Street, Suite 500
Grand Junction, CO 81501-2679
970.245.5811
http://www.lta.org/regionallta
index.html

Legacy Land Trust
P.O. Box 980816
Houston, TX 77098-0816
713.524.2100
http://www.llt.org/

Llano Estacado Audubon Society
P.O. Box 6066
Lubbock, TX 79493-6066
806.797.9562
http://www.leas.bizland.com/

The Nature Conservancy of Texas
P.O. Box 1440
711 Navarro
San Antonio, TX 78295-1440
210.224.8774
http://nature.org/wherewework/
northamerica/states/texas

The National Park Service,
Big Thicket
Big Thicket National Preserve
3785 Milam Street
Beaumont, TX 77701-4724
http://www.nps.gov/

The National Wildlife Federation
11100 Wildlife Center Drive
Reston, VA 20190-5362
800.822.9919
http://www.nwf.org/

Native Prairies Association of Texas
P.O. Box 210
Georgetown, TX 78627-0210
http://www.texasprairie.org/

Sierra Club, Lone Star Chapter
P.O. Box 1931
Austin, TX 78767
512.477.1729
http://www.texas.sierraclub.org/
contact.asp

Texas Parks and Wildlife Foundation
P.O. Box 191207 (75219)
1901 North Akard Street
Dallas, TX 75201
http://www.tpwf.org/

Texas Wildlife Association
401 Isom Road, Suite 237
San Antonio, TX 78216-5143
210.826.2904 or 800.839.9453
http://www.texas-wildlife.org/

Trust for Public Land
Texas State Office
815 Brazos Street, Suite 400
Austin, TX 78701
512.478.4644
http://www.tpl.org

U.S. Fish & Wildlife Service,
Southwest Region 2
500 Gold Avenue SW
Albuquerque, NM 87102
505-248-6911
http://southwest.fws.gov/

Valley Land Fund
2400 North 10th Street, Suite A
McAllen, TX 78501
http://www.valleylandfund.com/
conservation.html

Wetlands Habitat Alliance of Texas
118 East Hospital, Suite 208
Nacogdoches, TX 75961
800.962.9428
http://www.whatduck.org/

BIBLIOGRAPHY

Abernethy, Francis E. ed. *Tales from the Big Thicket*. Austin: University of Texas Press, 1966.

American Farmland Trust. "Going, Going, Gone: The impact of land fragmentation on Texas agriculture and wildlife." http://www.farmland.org/texas/frag_wildlife.htm

Amos, William H., and Stephen H. Amos. *Atlantic & Gulf Coasts: The Audubon Society Nature Guides*. New York: Chanticleer Press, 1985.

Austin American-Statesman, July 23, 1989. *Land Protection Plan for Lower Rio Grande Valley National Wildlife Refuge in Cameron, Hidalgo, Starr, and Willacy Counties, Texas*. Albuquerque: Southwest Region, U.S. Fish and Wildlife Service, January 1984, January 1985.

Bezanson, David, and David Wolfe. "Conservation Priorities for Texas: A Guide to Ten Threatened Areas in The Lone Star State." http://www.environmentaldefense.org/docments/1947_conserv4.pdf http://www.environmentaldefense.org/home.cfm

Bollaert, William. *William Bollaert's Texas*, Edited by W. Eugene Hollon and Ruth Lapham Butler. Norman: University of Oklahoma Press, 1956.

Britton, Joseph C., and Brian Morton. *Shore Ecology of the Gulf of Mexico*. Austin: University of Texas Press, 1989.

Brown, Lester R. *Eco-economy: Building an Economy for the Earth*. New York: W. W. Norton & Company, Inc., 2001.

Cohen, Rebecca S. "Texas by Georgia," *The Austin Chronicle Weekly Wire*. http://weeklywire.com/ww/03-23-98/austin_arts_feature1.html

Dale, Edward Everett. *The Cross-Timbers: Memories of a North Texas Boyhood*. Austin: University of Texas Press, 1966.

Deussen, Alexander. *Geology of the Coastal Plain of Texas*. Washington DC: U.S. Department of the Interior, 1924.

Diamond, David D., and Fred E. Smeins. "Composition, Classification, and Species Response Patterns of Remnant Tallgrass Prairies in Texas," *American Midland Naturalist* 113 (April 1985).

Diamond, David D. and Fred E. Smeins. "Remnant Grassland Vegetation and Ecological Affinities of the Upper Coastal Prairie of Texas," *Southwestern Naturalist* 29, August 28 (1984).

Everett, James H., and D. Lynn Drawe. *Trees, Shrubs and Cacti of South Texas*, Lubbock: Texas Tech University Press, 1993.

Flores, Dan. *Caprock Canyonlands*. Austin: University of Texas Press, 1990.

Fritz, Edward C. *The Wilderness Areas of East Texas*. Austin: University of Texas Press, 1986.

Fulmore, Zachary Taylor. *The Geography of Texas*. n.p.: Rand McNally, 1908.

Funk, Ben. "Hurricane!" *National Geographic,* September 1980.

Glover, William B. "A History of the Caddo Indians," *The Louisiana Historical Quarterly* 18, no. 4. (October, 1935). http://ops.tamu.edu/x075bb/caddo/Indians.html#I

Gould, Frank W. *The Grasses of Texas*. College Station: Texas A&M University Press, 1975.

Gunter, Pete A. Y. *The Big Thicket: An Ecological Reevaluation*. Denton: University of North Texas Press, 1993.

Hoese, H. Dickson, and Richard H. Moore. *Fishes of the Gulf of Mexico: Texas, Louisiana, and Adjacent Waters*. College Station: Texas A&M University Press, 1977.

Jameson, W. C. *Guadalupe Mountains: Island in the Desert*. El Paso: Texas Western Press, 1994.

Jordan, Terry G. "Perceptual Regions in Texas." *Geographical Review* 68 (July 1978).

———. "The Texan Appalachia." *Annals of the Association of American Geographers* 60 (September 1970).

———. *Texas: A Geography*. Boulder, CO: Westview Press, 1984.

Kramar, Stefan. *Stefan Kramar's Panhandle Portrait*. Austin: Pemberton Press, 1974.

Lewis, Willie Newbury. *Between Sun and Sod*. Clarendon: Clarendon Press, 1938; rev. ed., College Station: Texas A&M University Press, 1976.

Loughmiller, Campbell, and Lynn Loughmiller. *Big Thicket Legacy*. Austin: University of Texas Press, 1977.

Maxwell, Ross A. *Geologic and Historic Guide to the State Parks of Texas.* Bureau of Economic Geology, University of Texas at Austin, 1970.

MacMahon, James A. *Deserts, The Audubon Society Nature Guides.* New York: Chanticleer Press, 1985.

Myres, Samuel D. *The Permian Basin: Petroleum Empire of the Southwest.* El Paso: Permian Publishing, 1973, 1977.

Peacock, Howard. *The Big Thicket of Texas: America's Ecological Wonder.* Boston: Little, Brown, 1984.

Price, B. Byron and Frederick W. Rathjen. *The Golden Spread: An Illustrated History of Amarillo and the Texas Panhandle.* Northridge, CA: Windsor Publications, 1986.

Raht, Carlysle Grahm. *The Romance of the Davis Mountains and Big Bend Country.* Odessa, TX: The Rahtbooks Company, 1963.

Ramos, Mary G. editor. *The Texas Almanac.* Dallas: The Dallas Morning News, 1999.

Rathjen, Frederick W. *The Texas Panhandle Frontier.* Austin: University of Texas Press, 1973.

Schumacher, Robert W., et al. *Lower Rio Grande Valley National Wildlife Refuge Annual Narrative.* Alamo, TX: U.S. Department of the Interior, 1980–88.

Sellards, E. H., W. S. Adkins, and F. B. Plummer. *The Geology of Texas.* Austin: University of Texas Bulletin 3232, 1932.

Simonds, Frederic William. *Geographic Influences in the Development of Texas.* Austin: Journal of Geography, 1912.

Spearing, Darwin. *Roadside Geology of Texas.* Missoula, MT: Mountain Press, 1991.

Stambaugh, J. Lee, and Lillian J. *The Lower Rio Grande Valley of Texas.* San Antonio: Naylor, 1954.

Stanley, F. *Story of the Texas Panhandle Railroads.* Borger, TX: Hess Publishing Company, 1976.

Tennant, Alan. *The Guadalupe Mountains of Texas.* Austin: The University of Texas Press, 1980.

Texas Center for Policy Studies. *Texas Environmental Almanac*, 1995. http://www.texascenter.org/almanac/TXENVALMANAC.HTML

Texas Environmental Profiles, An Information and Online Activism Resource for the State of Texas. http://www.texasep.org

Texas State Historical Association. *The Handbook of Texas Online.* http://www.tsha.utexas.edu/handbook online/

Union Pacific Railroad Company, *The Resources and Attractions of the Texas Panhandle*: St. Louis: Woodward and Tiernan, 1891.

U.S. Environmental Protection Agency. "Global Warming" http://yosemite.epa.gov/OAR/globalwarming.nsf/content/ResourceCenterPublicationsSeaLevelRiseIndex.html

Warnock, Barton H. *Wildflowers of the Big Bend Country, Texas.* Alpine: Sul Ross State University, 1970.

Wauer, Roland H. *Naturalist's Big Bend.* College Station: Texas A&M University Press, 1983.

Nelson, Barney, editor. *God's Country or Devil's Playground. The Best Nature Writing from the Big Bend of Texas.* Austin: University of Texas Press, 2002.

Weaver, J. E., and F. W. Albertson. *Grasslands of the Great Plains.* Lincoln, NE: Johnsen Publishing Company, 1956.

Weddle, Robert S. *The French Thorn: Rival Explorers in the Spanish Sea, 1682–1762.* College Station: Texas A&M University Press, 1991.

Weddle, Robert S. *Spanish Sea: The Gulf of Mexico in North American Discovery, 1500–1685.* College Station: Texas A&M University Press, 1985.

Weniger, Del. *Cacti of Texas and Neighboring States.* Austin: The University of Texas Press, 1984.

West, Steve. *Northern Chihuahuan Desert Wildflowers.* Helena, MT: Falcon Publishing, in cooperation with the Carlsbad Caverns—Guadalupe Mountains Association, 2000.

McGowan, Brian J., and Brian K. Miller, and Clark D. McCreedy. "The Wildlife Habitat Incentives Program (WHIP) Can Help to Improve Wildlife Habitat." http://www.ces.purdue.edu/extmedia/FNR/FNR-168/FNR-168.html

Wilson, Edward O. *The Diversity of Life.* New York: W. W. Norton & Company, Inc., 1992.

Wilson, Steven C., and Karen C. Hayden. "Where Oil and Wildlife Mix," *National Geographic*, February 1981.

Gordon Young. "The Gulf's Workaday Waterway," *National Geographic*, February 1978.

Wright, Bill. *The Tiguas: Pueblo Indians of Texas.* El Paso: Texas Western Press, 1993.

New growth sprouts from the roots of a bare juniper tree,
Caprock Canyons State Park

ABOUT THE AUTHOR AND PHOTOGRAPHER

RICHARD REYNOLDS BECAME interested in photography in 1968 when he visited Big Bend National Park for the first time with a borrowed Kodak Signet 35mm camera. In 1973, he enrolled in Brooks Institute of Photography in Santa Barbara, California, where he received a degree in industrial photography and color technology in 1976. Between 1976 and 1983, Richard honed his skills as a landscape photographer. Following a seven-year stint as chief photographer for the Texas Tourist Development Agency and the Texas Department of Commerce, he began freelancing in 1990, specializing in scenes of Texas and the American Southwest.

His photographs have appeared in *National Geographic Traveler, Newsweek, Outside Magazine, Texas Monthly, Readers Digest,* and *Southern Living.* He is a regular contributor to *Texas Highways,* where he has more than twenty-five covers to his credit, and his work has appeared in dozens of calendars. He is also the photographer for nine other books: *Texas, Images of Wildness, Texas Reflections, Texas Wildflowers, Texas Hill Country, A Texas Christmas,* and *Texas, Then & Now,* (all by Westcliffe Publishers), and *Texas Wildflowers, Texas Impressions*, and *Big Bend Impressions* (Far Country Press). He and his wife, Nancy, now make their home in Austin.